# The Matchbook

## and

## Other Cop Stories

### by Eli J. Miletich

ISBN: 1-4107-1695-3 (e-book)
ISBN: 1-4107-1696-1 (Paperback)

Library of Congress Control Number: 2003090396


This book is printed on acid free paper.


Printed in the United States of America
Bloomington, IN


1stBooks - rev. 6/25/03

*For My Teachers, Violet Nelson,*

*Ross Ewoldsen, Waldemar Johnson,*

*Ray Mickolajak, Walt Hunting, Callie Merritt,*

*and all the other people who encouraged me*

*during my formative years.*

*and*

*For my wife, Carol,*

*Who always inspires me*

*and*

*Stacy, Dana and Derek*

# PREFACE

In police work, those involved see a wide range of human experiences, many repeated over and over, from traffic violators to thieves, burglars, rapists, robbers and murderers.

In my thirty three year career with the Duluth, Minnesota Police Department and one year spent in Bosnia, once a part of the former Yugoslavia, I saw and was involved in either investigating or reviewing the work of others in that arena often called 'Cops and Robbers'.

In the police service there are generally three categories of police work, i.e., Patrol, Investigations and Management. In working in those capacities I learned much, not only about law enforcement but about humanity.

An officer working as a Patrolman on regular squad duty, and being the usual first responder, he or she is exposed to those incidents of mankinds emotional and mental lapses and failures. Of all, rape, suicide and homicide can leave the deepest scars on an officer, even the most outwardly toughest. Those were exciting, but traumatic days.

Working in investigations and later as an administrator, I also saw the how the public demands perfection from those they entrust to their safety but at most times will hesitate, if not refuse, to support those folks who are out there putting their lives on the line for them. It was even more obvious after I had advanced to the position of Police Chief.

It is said, by so called learned and intelligent people, that most of us are products of our environment, i.e., family, schools, church, neighborhood; but mostly the family.

There were nine kids in our family. All, except one, matriculated to very productive lives, and even he was on a path in that direction when fate took a hand in his life.

Nick, one of my older brothers, was also influenced by conditions and occurrences outside the immediate family. He subsequently spent almost half of his short life of thirty eight years in a variety of penal institutions. He finally became determined that he was going to straighten out his life and, in managing a resort in Michigan's upper peninsula for over two years prior to his death, appeared to have done so. He died in a car accident at thirty eight years of age.

A commentary on his behalf is that in todays society he would not have served time for his initial offenses, rather, he would have been viewed as an example of a misunderstood youth.

In the seventh grade at West Junior High in 1940, he didn't correctly respond to the disciplinary practices of that era. He was frequently engaged in verbal sparring with his teachers and saw fit to challenge one, a Miss Johnson, who pulled his hair when she wanted his attention. Talking back, sassing, they called it.

After several infractions he was taken to Juvenile Court and judged to be incorrigible. He was sentenced to the Boys State Reformatory at Red Wing, Minnesota, across the state about two hundred miles from his home and family. He was 12 years old. His first offense, if you will. His parents had not been permitted to speak at his hearing. I recall to this day hearing our mother crying, wailing, throughout the night when she and our father returned home from that experience in Juvenile Court. Throughout the years, even though she had more or less been toughened by his escapades, his death in a car accident brought about the same emotions in her.

The education he received at Red Wing far surpassed anything he would have learned in the public schools. He learned several fine arts.

He learned how to con people. He learned how to pick locks. He learned how to sign other peoples names as well, or better than those who owned the names. This is not to say that I am apologizing for him, because his siblings did not fall into that same pattern, but it was another indicator of what the system can do to an individual if he is caught up in the whirlpool of corruption.

Our late brother, Dr. Steve, the eldest of the boys, had retired after 39 years as a professor at the University of Minnesota, Minneapolis, and his student prodigies are all around the country, Europe as well. Gloria is a Registered Nurse, who also found time to raise a family. Another deceased brother, Marty, was the State of Minnesota Supervisor of Drivers License Examiners. Our youngest brother, Tom, retired as a Navy Chief after twenty one years on nuclear submarines, tested for police officer in Pascagoula, Mississippi, and is a Captain on that department. Eva, now retired, was a regional manager for a national insurance company in Dallas, Texas. Sisters Mary, the family's eldest who died of cancer, and Goldie, successfully raised families before going back into the work force. The nine kids of Ilija and Italika Miletich, immigrants from Croatia.

As for myself, when I graduated from high school, police work didn't even remotely receive consideration as an occupational choice. I volunteered for the military draft at eighteen, served two years, and was with the Army in Germany in the last year of U.S. occupation of that defeated nation. Returning, I attended the University of Minnesota, Duluth, played on the football team and worked toward a degree in political science. I must admit though, that while academics were on the agenda, football and playing hockey in the winter for a strong Chun King Oriental's semi pro hockey team were foremost on my mind.

Taking a patrolman's exam which was recently posted by the City of Duluth Civil Service Office, as suggested by several of my teammates, brought a laugh from me, though I did join three others in filling out applications.

I had strong reservations about taking a job even if I was successful and a position offered, though it was pretty well known that another West Duluth man, Chief Walter Wiski, had been doing a yeoman's job in straightening out the department with firm but fair discipline.

Additionally, several older guys from 'the Street' were now in law enforcement in the area, Rod Skorich, Al Senarighi, Charlie Pavlich, Emil Carich, Pete Kurtovich, George Ujdur, with the St. Louis County Sheriff's Department; Steve Kurtovich, Walt Zivkovich and Dan Price with the Duluth Police Department and, of course, the guy who broke ground for us all, John Stanco, who began with the Department in the late thirties.

Was law enforcement being infiltrated by guys with funny sounding surnames?

The written exam was given on a Saturday morning to one hundred ninety applicants. That it was on a Saturday was fortunate for those UMD students taking the exam as we didn't have to cut classes to be there.

A physical fitness test followed and that helped weed out some of the aspiring cops,

The results were mailed to us several weeks later. I scored third overall, but my three teammates didn't pass. Don't anyone be fooled by that though, because written exams are not the only gauge to determine if one is fit for any job or position, some people are just not test persons. One of my former teammates who took the test in now a vice president of one of the state of Georgia's largest banks. Another is an executive with the 3 M Company. One was a successful attorney, now deceased.

After a short spell I was called for an interview with the Chief and his staff and subsequently hired.

I later met for coffee with two of the guys from 'the Street' who had been on the job since the early fifties, Steve Kurtovich and Walt Zivkovich.

"Look, Eli, the job, like any other, is what you make of it," said Walt, now a retired teacher and school counselor in the local school system, "Sure, the department went through some tough times, but that was just a reflection of society as a whole. When you're hired, do your job, and do it better than anyone else. Keep your nose clean, don't drink on the job, don't carouse and things will go okay."

"That's about it," agreed Steve, adding, "and don't take any shit from some of the older guys who still look at us as 'the dumb hunkies from Raleigh Street.' There aren't too many of them left on the job, but they still carry a lot of weight, so watch your back!"

Good advice from two good friends.

Our families were long time close friends, since the earlier immigration of our parents from Yugoslavia, and in all the years since. That really can't be explained so that a person can understand it without having lived it.

I started on the Duluth Police Department Training School as a twenty three year old on a cold January 2, 1959, determined that I would do my part in law enforcement, as well as to help eliminate the abuses by the police which I was familiar with from the past though, as noted earlier, the department had been cleaned up considerably since Walt Wiski had been appointed Chief several years before.

This story highlights a homicide case as mysterious and dramatic as any I've seen or heard of and also describes some of my experiences in thirty three years of police work, trying to make a difference.

I will stress that though the happenings as told herein are true, the names of _some_ of the actors have been altered or changed outright, because I've always believed that we are not our brothers keeper and I don't want to cause any undue discomfort or embarrassment to survivors or relatives of those folks involved in these incidents. That selective censoring choice is mine, since the typewriter also belongs to me. :-)

Chapter One

## October 1

The early fall thunderstorm blew in from the northwest with a sudden fury in the middle of the afternoon, not too much unlike a hurricane, dropping over two inches of rain in less than one hour.

The rain was accompanied by wind and golf ball size hail so nasty that motorists were forced to pull off the road wherever they may be, on city street, alley or interstate freeway.

At about the peak of the storm several motorists, who had stopped on the shoulder of Arrowhead Road to wait out the worst, noticed something on the other side of the roadside ditch in the high brown grass which had been blown over, almost flat, by the force of the torrential storm.

Arrowhead Road, in the northwest corner of the city of Duluth, is a busy thoroughfare which connects the neighborhoods of Kenwood and Duluth Heights. It also is one of the feeder routes for the nearby campuses of the University of Minnesota, Duluth, and the College of St. Scholastica. Roads

*Eli J. Miletich*

spinning off to the Duluth International Airport also intersect

with Arrowhead.

As the storm subsided, one of the curious motorists left his

car for a closer look at the object and found a quilt wrapped

around what appeared to be a human body, with legs

protruding from one end, wearing what appeared to be black

slacks or trousers. Whether it was a young male or a small

female could not be determined.

"Call the police," he hollered to no one in particular.

When the "Body found in a ditch" call was transmitted by the

police radio dispatcher, a St. Louis County Sheriff's Deputy, out

serving papers, happened to be in the neighborhood and

decided to stop by to see if he could be of some help. Fat

chance! He could have botched it. Crime scene preservation is

not one of the Sheriff's Department strong suits. But, when

serving subpoenas and warrants are your major functions and

your county commissioners appropriate virtually nothing for

training, what more can be expected?

Arriving at the scene ahead of the dispatched city squad,

the deputy apparently became just another curious tourist.

Several occupants of other vehicles, stranded by the sudden storm, were out and around the body, not concerned about what evidence, if any might be trampled into the ground. The deputy joined right in with them, circling the body a couple times so that when the police arrived, a flattened circle was visible around the victim.

The next cop to arrive was an out of shape, pigeon toed, prematurely balding sergeant, Ben France. Not one to take intelligent command, but seeing what was happening to the scene, he dourly said, "Let's clear away from the body so that the Identification Tech's can try to make some sense of all this." With that, he returned to his car, called communications and asked that a detective be sent, as well as an I.D. Technician.

Keeping true to form, he questioned no one, rather, just waited like the other passers by.

In the next two minutes more help arrived, Detective Bureau Shift Commander Lieutenant John Hall and one of his sergeants, Ross Browne, as well as an I.D. Tech, a patrolman named Rivers.

*Eli J. Miletich*

Lieutenant Hall had called Detective Bureau Inspector Fred Sowl from the scene on Arrowhead Road to advise him that it appeared the dead woman was wrapped in a quilt, with some obvious injuries visible about the head. He was sure it was a homicide and not some poor, confused soul who had wandered out of her home one night, laid down to rest, and died. He added that he was going to assign Sergeant Browne to coordinate the investigation.

Inspector Sowl buzzed me on the phone for a briefing and when he advised me of Hall's pending assignment of Browne to the case, he received a negative response. "No way." I exclaimed into the phone. "Pardon," said the soft spoken, easy going Sowl.

"Fred, you know what I think of the way that guy has handled a couple of the homicide cases he's worked on in the last ten years. He's one of the worst wheel spinners on the whole damn department, going nowhere fast, but always trying to give an impression that he is being productive," I stressed, "in the meantime, he hasn't been available for assignment to other cases, and he's been shielded from open criticism by the

4

previous department administration. No, no way am I going to okay this!"

"Who do you suggest then, Chief?" came back Fred.

"In my opinion Dick Yagoda and Pat Alexander are the most persistent and street wise investigators we've got since Dan Price retired.

The others are good, but on this one, with no identification on the body, no suspects, no witnesses, I want someone who will push for quick accurate answers and not be content to dictate notes and memos into a small recorder, then play back its contents endlessly for the next three years, listening for something which he may have omitted or overlooked. Sharing information with no one. In the meantime, the body gets buried, important questions go unanswered and we end up with an unsolved homicide."

"Yagoda's busy on another case, but how about I assign Alexander to coordinate, with Yagoda committed to assisting whenever he can? We can also use the guys in I.D. for whatever Alexander decides," said Sowl.

*Eli J. Miletich*

"Good," I said, "you know, Fred, I don't like to micro manage day to day assignments, but when we're talking about a homicide, I need to look at the track records of the guys involved, just like a baseball manager looks at the won-loss records of his pitchers when it comes to crucial games, and the bottom line is that the ultimate responsibility comes down to me."

Sowl, sounding just a bit dejected, said, "Yes, I know, and I'll try to get Hall to see it that way. By the way, do you want to be kept up to date if anything develops?"

"You bet!"

Chapter Two

Sergeant Patrick Alexander was a twenty two year veteran of the Duluth Police Department and a very likable guy with a disarming smile. With almost coal black hair and mustache going with a dark, olive, complexion fitting for one of mixed Greek and Croatian heritage he most always caught the eye of women in a restaurant or bar when he walked into such places. Because he also had a more than slight resemblance to folk singer Slim Whitman, his nickname was appropriately "Slim".

Alexander had been raised in the Helm Street neighborhood in the West End of town which had a mixed bag of ethnic groups ranging from Italian to Russian and from Greek to Swedish, first generation at that, so it provided for some interesting developing years.

As in any such neighborhood in the forties, the memories were of raiding gardens, apple trees, and sometimes such places as nearby scrap yards.

One of his favorite boyhood yarns was of the time he and buddies Paully and Jim, at around eight or nine years of age

7

*Eli J. Miletich*

and looking for something to ride around on, their families couldn't afford to buy wagons which kids in some of the more affluent communities had, so they visited the scrap yard and found just the right thing.

It was as if their prayers had been answered. A huge brass bed, intact, with wheels and curved headboard loomed before them.

Whatever the providential reason, the bed had not been fed into the cutter yet, so they claimed it for their own, wheeling it out of the yard as if they had just purchased it, past scrap yard workers who paid them no mind.

On Michigan Street, a thoroughfare in their neighborhood, en route to one of their homes, they came across a police squad.

When stopped by the officers, they were not asked any questions about ownership of the bed, rather, the cops were concerned that they may hit a parked car, causing damage, thus making work for them. "Get that damn thing off the road, and right now," one of the cops said as they rode off.

When Alexander was appointed to the police department, he retained that little lesson in life, among many others from his upbringing, that the police had made a mistake in asking no questions. He quickly established himself as one of the brightest, hardest working and productive of the whole department. He asked questions and never accepted what, to others, might appear obvious until he had approached it from all possible angles.

---

When told of his assignment to the suspected homicide, Alexander immediately took charge, telling I.D. Tech Rivers, over police radio, to wait until he arrived at the scene before checking for possessions on the body or in the clothes. He also directed Sergeant Ross Browne to start questioning all who were at the scene, additionally telling France to resume whatever he was doing before he came there. He thought, "If I ask him to do anything, it might be weeks before I see a completed report, or he'll just screw it up anyway. Better he's the hell out of the way."

With the finders of the body hustled off about fifty feet from the immediate scene for preliminary questioning by Browne and another detective who had arrived, Alexander and Rivers then proceeded to unravel the body from the quilt, making an effort to keep the body in the same position it was lying in when found. They saw that it was a young woman wearing black slacks, a black sweater with a pattern of glass beads sewn around the collar, and shoes. Her head was a mass of blood and appeared to have been struck many times with a blunt object. She was not wearing a jacket or coat. Odd for that time of year in Duluth? It was thirty eight degrees Fahrenheit at 3:30 P.M. Alexander noticed a break in the sweaters' glass bead pattern around the neck, as if one or more of the beads were missing.

She was not adorned in any of the other items that might be found on a young female. No bracelet. No Necklace. No earrings. No purse. But most important, No identification!

"What's that?" Alexander asked Rivers who had removed a small object from the right front pocket of the slacks.

"Not much, just a book of matches," was the answer.

"Let's see," said Alexander, "Is there any writing on it?"

"Yeah, looks like an ordinary matchbook from some bar in a town in Colorado," Rivers maintained, "millions of these kind of matchbooks in existence."

"Well, why don't you make out a property report, place it an an evidence container, and we'll see if it can help us in any way," said Alexander. "Get photos of this scene from all angles and from different distances, then let's have her brought to the morgue to see if the Medical Examiner can give us any help with this," adding, "It sure doesn't look like this thing took place here, no sign of a scuffle and from the way her head is battered, there should be some sign of blood around but there's none. Do a thorough search of the entire scene."

Alexander mulled over the lack of identity and, because she appeared to be in her early to mid twenties, could she be a student at the University of Minnesota, Duluth, or St. Scholastica? Because she had a light brown tone to her skin, was she of Native American, Latin or Mideast background? Was there a missing person report on file on her?

At the morgue, the Deputy Medical Examiner got to work right away. With the precision and intensity of one of Boris Karloff's characters from a thirties horror movie, he began the work that they, Medical Examiners, excel in, that is, determine the cause and approximate time of death.

Dr. Don Atteli had a reputation among his peers as one of the tops in the state, if not the Midwest. He worked his way through college and medical school driving over the road tractor trailers, eighteen wheelers as they're known in the trade, for Michelina's Frozen Dinners, owned by Duluthian Jeno Paulucci. Michelina's is one of the largest manufactures of frozen Italian foods in the country and its owner a fiery, tough, guy to work for, treated those who put in a good days effort like one of his family.

While going through his medical schooling, Atteli used to boast to his fellow students about driving the tractor-trailers, "I'm in an elite group of over the road drivers who have put on over a million miles in the big one and never had an accident."

Though Jeno and Atteli had only met a couple times, Jeno meticulously read employee evaluation reports. He employs over one thousand at several locations around the country and he frequently told his managers that here was a young man who was going to amount to something. No one could have been prouder than Jeno when Atteli completed medical school.

Deputy Medical Examiner Atteli, (the State of Minnesota had discarded the old Coroner system and moved to a Medical Examiner several years before), after approximately an hour and forty five minutes, gave Alexander his preliminary findings.

The victim had died from a crushed skull, caused by more than five blows delivered with a heavy blunt object. A broken finger, broken fingernails and abrasions on her right hand, indicated that she had put up a fight.

Atteli, thorough as ever, when checking the clean white sheet in which the body was brought to the morgue, had noticed two small strands of hair which seemed not to be from the victim and he called this to Alexanders attention.

"Are you sure these are not from the victims body?" queried Alexander.

"Only a lab test will tell us that," replied Dr. Atteli, "but you will notice that her hair is jet black, and these two strands are a lighter shade of brown. They also appear to be cranial hair."

"She has been dead at least two days." concluded Atteli.

Alexander received the two pieces of hair from the doctor and placed them in a glassine bag, sealing the opening. He initialed the label on the outside of the bag, placed the time and date and asked Atteli to initial the package as well. This would be shipped to the State Crime Laboratory.

Returning to headquarters, Alexander found his desk in-basket containing several reports from Sergeant Browne reference the people he had interviewed at the Arrowhead Road location. They all had the same basic stuff. Pulling over during the storm, they noticed the object in the bent over high grass on the other side of the ditch. One driver who was watching when Alexander and Rivers had uncovered the body, was an anthropology student at UMD and he offered an opinion that the victim appeared to be of Middle East origin.

Lieutenant Beverly Ecklund, the day shift Detective Bureau officer-in-charge, related that campus police had been contacted at both UMD and St. Scholastica as well as across the bay at the University of Wisconsin, Superior, and they were checking with housing and dormitory officials for any reported missing students. "It may take a few days."

"We also have contacted a number of stores and chain operations in town which are on the Check Alert program to see if anyone recognized her by the description we provided, but Duluth is stretched out so far that may take time too."

This was the initial stage of the second investigation of the death of a woman to be coordinated by Sergeant Pat Alexander.

## Chapter Three

One day, about ten years earlier, in the Narco Vice office, I was startled out of a day dream at my typewriter.

"Hey, Eli!" shouted Pat Alexander, while he was browsing through the Duluth News Tribune, "did you see where Jim Grebbs' wife died? She was pretty young."

"I just heard a couple weeks ago that they were going through a divorce," I said, "what did she die from?"

"I'm just reading the obituary, and it doesn't say the cause of death."

'Why don't you check with Sandy at the Coroner's office?'" I asked Pat, who was as curious as I, in that we knew her husband, Jim, an attorney, was only 38 or 39 years old himself. We really didn't know his wife, but had seen her a time or two and she was a striking beauty who appeared in excellent health, at least outwardly.

That afternoon Pat got a return call from Sandy Sterling, secretary at the Coroner's office and he learned that Shirley Grebbs had died in the office of Dr. Stan Gutenberg, a local

The Matchbook and Other Cop Stories

psychiatrist. Also that the Deputy Coroner's completed report form indicated that she had died of natural causes.

"Wow!" I exclaimed.

"Yeah, wow!" echoed Pat. We both had immediately recalled an incident over a year previous, involving the good Dr. Gutenberg. We were not involved, nor did we assist in that case, but anyone working investigations on the department was fully aware of what happened on a crisp October evening at the doctor's office.

---

About a year before Mrs. Grebbs death, at about 7:30 P.M. on a Wednesday night, a certain John Diller came in to Police Headquarters and asked to speak to a detective.

The desk officer directed him to the Detective Bureau where he was in turn sent to the desk of Sergeants Dwight Saaf and Fred Sowl.

Both were experienced cops, assigned to the Detective Bureau, having worked in virtually every unit of the department. They were very knowledgeable and street wise.

*Eli J. Miletich*

Saaf with twenty years and Sowl, over twelve on the department, had worked the broad spectrum of cases a city police department would be involved in. In other words, they've been there.

"My wife, Lucy, had a doctor's appointment for 4:45 this afternoon. She didn't come home and I don't know where she might be."

"Who is her doctor, and did you call his office?" asked Sowl.

"Her doctor is Gutenberg, Stan Gutenberg, a psychiatrist. I called there about six P.M. and there was no answer."

Saaf, always the calm gentleman, offered, "Well, maybe when she finished at the doctor's office, she went shopping. You know, a lot of the downtown stores are open later now, and the malls are open 'till 9:30."

"No, I checked the Fourth Avenue Parking Ramp, where she parks when she goes to the doctor. You can get free parking by just having the doctor's receptionist stamp the parking ticket. Anyway, her car is still there," he said.

"I also checked the basement level parking where the doctors and other professionals park. Dr. Gutenberg's car is still

18

there. I'm afraid something has happened to her or maybe even both of them."

Sowl then suggested, "Could it be possible that she met a sister or a close friend and they went somewhere like a movie or for a cup of coffee and a bite to eat?"

"No, that's not like her, she always lets me know when she's going to be somewhere other than where she is scheduled to be. Besides, I went to the Medical Arts Building and a janitor was cleaning up the lobby, the main floor door was not locked, so I went right in, caught the elevator to the third floor, Dr. Gutenberg's floor. I could see right through the clear glass entry door and the office was dark, except for the corridor that leads away to the rear of the receptionists desk where I saw a light under a door down that hall. I think it was one of the patient visiting rooms."

"Did you try the door, or knock?" queried Saaf.

"No, I was afraid something had happened. I came straight up to your office," he replied, "I was able to walk into that building and the janitor did not say a word. Any nut could do the same thing. You know, some of his patients have serious

19

problems and I'm sure that some could get violent. And, there are a lot of other medical offices in that building. I just don't know."

"Why don't we go down there," suggested Saaf, "maybe there is a simple answer to all this."

At the Medical Arts Building they found the lobby door unlocked and the janitor just finishing up his chores.

After the detectives had identified themselves, Saaf asked the janitor to accompany them to the third floor. If the doctors office was locked, they would want him to use his master key to let them in. They knew their action would be appropriate in view of the possibility that someone might be hurt, or worse, in that office.

Stepping off the elevator they turned left, walked down the hall, passing several other medical offices until they stood in front of Gutenberg's door which was glass with a wood frame.

Like John Diller, they could see a light coming from under a door about half way down a long corridor within the office.

When Saaf tried the door handle it turned, and when he gently pushed, it opened. They thanked the janitor and he returned to his duties.

All the lights in the entire outer office and corridor were off, so they paused a couple seconds to get accustomed to the dark, then proceeded to the room with the light showing through at the bottom.

When Saaf tried the door, it opened and there before them was the good Dr. Stan Gutenberg standing in front of an examining table in just his boxer shorts, clearly aroused.

Lying on the examining table, completely nude, and obviously in an unconscious state, was John Diller's wife, Lucy. An embarrassed John Diller quickly and silently backed out into the corridor.

"Oh, my god, oh my god, what have I done. There goes my practice. I don't know what I was doing, " breathed the good doctor, heavily.

After he took a sheet from a cabinet and covered Lucy, and then unsuccessfully tried to wake her, Saaf turned to Gutenberg. "Doctor, get dressed, we want to talk to you but first, tell us what you administered to her to make her sleep so soundly?"

"I had put her into a restful state with sodium pentothal so I could work with her on something that is troubling her from her past. I don't know what came over me. She is a very attractive woman."

"How long before she wakes up?" asked Sowl.

"In about another fifteen or twenty minutes."

"Good, you come down the hall with us where we can talk. We'll have Mr. Diller come down here and get her undergarments and clothes on her and he can wait with her while we talk," directed Saaf.

"Doctor," asked Sowl when they had reached another room, "please tell us just what was going on in there?"

"I've never done anything like this before, you've got to believe me. I was just overcome by her beauty and lost my mind. I'm 49 years old and have a spotless record, and a good reputation in my professional field. When she was lying there, I knew she was going to be sleeping for another forty five minutes or so, so I decided to have sex with her. I didn't do anything before you got here, thankfully. Pentothal is used in therapy as well as an anesthetic for surgery. It is commonly called a truth serum."

"She knew you were giving her pentothal, but did she consent to this act, doctor?" asked Sowl.

"Well, no, but I might have told her later."

"Are you married doctor?" Saaf inquired.

"Yes, we have three children. Please don't let my wife know about this," he begged, "this is really a private matter."

Sowl interjected. "Attempting to have sex with a sleeping woman, not your wife, put to sleep by an injection of sodium pentothal administered by you, no, that is not a private matter. Doctor, you're a professional man and I'm sure that the State Medical Board of Professional Conduct prohibits such conduct, as well."

"What are you going to do with me now?" Gutenberg asked.

Dwight Saaf answered. "We are going to prepare reports and refer the matter to the County Attorney's office, requesting prosecution. We also are going to recommend that copies of

23

our reports be forwarded to the State Medical Board for their review and action.

"Doctor," added Sowl, "I'd suggest that you go home and tell your wife of this matter, it's better that she hears it first from you."

"We're going to assist Mr. Diller with his wife now," said Saaf. " I'd suggest that you wait in this room until they have gone to their car."

"Okay."

When they returned to the first room, they found Lucy awake, but a bit groggy. John Diller said that he would leave her car in the parking ramp and drive her home in his vehicle.

Sergeant Saaf advised him of the action the department would be taking.

"Do you think that I should contact an attorney?" Diller asked them.

"That's a decision that you must make, Mr. Diller," answered Sergeant Sowl, "If you do retain an attorney, our reports will be available for him as they are a matter of public record."

In the ensuing days, the County Attorney's office prosecution team decided that there wasn't a strong enough case for criminal prosecution, but they did indicate that they would forward all reports to the State Medical Board of Professional Conduct.

It was during that time that the attorney representing Doctor Gutenberg began visiting the County Attorney's office, seeking to convince them that this was a one time lapse in judgment and conduct by his client. "It had never happened before, and it would never happen again. He has been a valued member of the community and it would be devastating to have him disciplined for this incident."

After several weeks of such conversations, Dr. Gutenberg's attorney won out. He saved the good doctor's hide. The decision was to hold the reports in abeyance and, if any other similar information comes to the forefront, take appropriate action then. Naturally, the police department wasn't happy.

John Diller had subsequently initiated civil court action, charging the good doctor with alienation of affection. That lawsuit was ultimately settled out of court and no amount was publicly disclosed, although rumor had it around $15,000. There was no publicity, negative or otherwise.

Oh, by the way, the attorney representing the good doctor in all aspects of this case was Jim Grebbs.

———————————

Here we were, one year later, discussing the death of Shirley Grebbs, which death had occurred in that same Dr. Gutenberg's office.

"Pat, I think we need to do a couple things to satisfy our curiosity about this thing. One, let's get in touch with the Deputy Coroner, Dr. Engston, and find out from him what led him to believe that Shirley Grebbs died of natural causes. Second, we need to talk with the good Dr. Gutenberg and ask him what took place in his office prior to her death."

"Got it," said Pat Alexander, "I'm also going to try to talk with Gutenberg's receptionist, and nurse, if he has one. I think they might provide us with a little insight. And I want to make sure that I talk with them when the doctor is busy with a patient. Also, when I talk with Dr. Engston I'm going to ask him if he knows why the police weren't notified to respond to the death of Mrs. Grebbs.

We all know that a police squad should be summoned to instances of death in public as well as private facilities other than a hospital. Something just doesn't look right here."

"Go to it, Pat. The rest of the guys in the office will carry on with the Narco-Vice stuff that might come in for you so that you have time to look into this. I'll let Inspector Barber know what's up. It may be that we're just overly suspicious here, but it's better to check it out than to be in doubt the rest of our lives. Inspector Barber just may want to assign someone from the Detective Bureau if it turns out to be something that needs further looking into, but in the meantime, start it off."

In two days, Alexander learned, according to the psychiatrists receptionist that the death of Shirley Grebbs occurred after she had suffered a severe reaction to an injection of sodium pentothal which the doctor had given her when she came in for her regular bimonthly therapy appointment. She had been seeing the psychiatrist for about three months.

27

While lying on the examination table after the injection, she had begun to choke, making gurgling sounds as if suffocating. The doctor reacted by administering sodium amytal, a relative of pentothal, which the doctor thought would bring her out of the reaction she was suffering. Instead, she worsened.

The doctor checked his oxygen supply and found out that his supply, a small tank, was empty. He said that he ran down a stairway rather than wait for an elevator, the building is fourteen stories, with a battery of four elevators, and he didn't want to wait, so he took the stairs for the three flights to ground level where the pharmacy was located.

At the pharmacy, he asked for and received a fresh tank. He then ran up the same stairwell but when he reached the room the patient was in, she was dead.

The good doctor called the Coroner's office and the staff there called Dr. Engston, a Deputy Coroner, who in turn went to the psychiatrists office to check the deceased.

Gutenberg told Engston what happened and he agreed that it must have been a reaction to the pentothal thus, death by natural causes. He accepted Gutenberg's story and signed off just below the psychiatrists signature, but did say that he had checked Mrs. Grebbs underpants to see if they were wet. Did he know of the psychiatrists perversions?

Sergeant Alexander also learned from the receptionist that she did not know of Mrs. Grebbs difficulty until the doctor returned from the pharmacy with the oxygen tank. He had not called out for help.

Dr. Engston could not offer a rational explanation as to his reasons for accepting the psychiatrist's story, except that he was a fellow medical professional. For that same reason, he felt comfortable in signing the death certificate. He did not think to call the police department to have officers sent to the scene. In retrospect, he felt he should have reacted differently. How nice!

Because the victim had died in other than a hospital, an examination of her stomach contents and blood were performed by a pathologist at the morgue. The sodium pentothal and sodium amytal were readily determined to be present in strong doses in her blood.

A new factor arose with the discovery of undigested tablets of Valium, a strong sedative, in her stomach.

*Eli J. Miletich*

When we received the preliminary report on that, Pat Alexander went to Gutenberg's office to inquire about the Valium.

"Oh yes," Gutenberg said, "I had given her a prescription for that several weeks ago. She was having a hard time sleeping at night, so I thought that would help. But that wouldn't have caused her to have a reaction."

Alexander had been doing some digging through other sources and found out that for the past several years the doctor had been suspected of using pentothal for his lustful purposes with a small number of other female patients, this in addition to Mrs. Lucy Diller. Pat set out to check this further.

In the meantime, I briefed Inspector Russ Barber that there was a possibility that there was more to the good doctor's activities than meets the eye. Did he want to have someone else in the Detective Bureau pick up the case? "No, Pat has done a great job on it thus far, let's let him go as far with it as possible.

By the way, because of the connection that at least one member of the County Attorney's staff has with the deceased's

30

husband, I think we had better play this close to the vest until we have enough to make a move. Otherwise we could risk him being tipped off. And it's still not clear how she came to be a patient of the doctor is it?"

"Okay, Inspector, we'll keep all our reports in our confidential file 'till we're ready to move, if there in fact is a move to make. And you're right, we don't know how that doctor-patient relationship came to pass, especially since the husband, estranged or not, should have remembered what kind of a lecherous scoundrel the doctor is."

With several names furnished to him by confidential sources, Pat Alexander made contact with each, two women from Duluth and one woman from an Iron Range mining town of Northeastern Minnesota.

All had almost identical stories.

They were patients of the doctor because of an emotional or stressful situation they had found themselves in. As patients of the doctor, he had commenced treatment with a prescription of Valium. Then, because he wanted to get to the root cause of their problem, he started with sodium pentothal therapy.

Each one, they were interviewed separately and didn't know the others, stated that they thought the doctor may have molested them sexually, even intercourse, during pentothal treatment. Reasons for their suspicions were given as being wet and sore in the vaginal area after therapy treatments. Because he was a professional medical person, each felt guilty about thinking this way and wrote it off as a manifestation of their personal stress.

The abrupt cancellation of further appointments by one, then another, then later, the last one, caused one of the office staff to call the patient from the Iron Range. She learned of the woman's suspicions and the guilt feelings for having thought that the doctor could have done so, but the lingering doubt and suspicion kept her from making further appointments.

When Alexander told me of this latest bit of information, I said that we need to talk further with our boss, Inspector Barber, and see what he might suggest.

Barber, the old pro, thought that we should try to set up a meeting with one of the foremost forensic pathologists in the state, Dr. Robert Hanft, of the Hennepin County Medical

Examiners Office, in Minneapolis, give him what we have, and see what he has to offer. Again, not that staff and personnel of our county coroner's office were not to be trusted, but local confidentially was one way of preserving this investigation until the proper time.

Russ Barber, the guy to whom county and city prosecutors came for advice, the guy who was a walking encyclopedia of criminals and criminal activity in the upper Midwest, was well respected in the law enforcement community, thus when he called Dr. Hanft, he got right through.

"Russ, can you send me the autopsy report?" said Dr. Hanft. "This looks a bit peculiar to me, but, of course, I'd like to know more about what killed her. It still could have been natural causes, you know."

To Barber, it sounded like the pathologist was not going to give a prejudicial opinion. However his "peculiar" comment indicated he was indeed interested.

"Sure," responded Barber, "we have copies on hand and we'll have them in the mail to you in a matter of minutes."

Two days later Dr. Hanft called.

"Russ, this is Bob Hanft. I think that you guys may have something up there. The fact that this gal was on Valium, prescribed by the psychiatrist, should have ruled out his use of pentothal therapy unless he was absolutely positive that she had not taken Valium that day. He should have instructed her in that. But to administer the pentothal without being sure could be lethal much less, administer amytal on top of it. I'd suggest that we try to set up a meeting with the Chief of Psychiatry at the University of Minnesota School of Medicine. He's a friend named Bob Peterson and he's been Chief over there for about twenty five years, and one hell of a straight shooter."

"Can you contact him and make the arrangements if he is amenable to a meeting?" asked Barber, "on any day that's compatible to the both of you, we can come down to the Twin Cities."

"I think that in both our cases a Saturday will be best, but I'll call him and get back to you," said Hanft.

The next day, a Tuesday, Dr. Hanft called and said that an appointment was made to meet on the following Saturday, nine in the morning in Dr. Peterson's conference room at the University.

Driving to Minneapolis on Saturday, Inspector Barber cautioned Pat Alexander and me not to be too optimistic about what we might learn at the meeting, "But on the other hand, they must think there are possibilities or we wouldn't be going to any meeting with these two guys. I'm sure they've got better things to do on a nice Saturday morning than look at goofy theories of a few cops from Duluth."

After introductions all around, we laid out the information we had brought along, verbally as well as in written report form.

Dr. Peterson explained that he had had an opportunity to review the autopsy report and explained that Dr. Gutenberg had been a student of his "about fifteen, maybe seventeen years ago."

He said, "Sodium pentothal should only be administered under the most guarded conditions. By that, I mean that a physician should make sure that no other sedatives, or drugs of any kind, have been consumed by the patient prior to the use of pentothal. Also, there should be a nurse in attendance to assist.

35

*Eli J. Miletich*

A full supply of oxygen needs to be available in the same room in which the pentothal is administered.

Additionally, sodium amytal should not be administered on top of pentothal, particularly if there is any kind of reaction to the first drug. The drugs are related, thus, to use one and then the other, is only compounding any problem which the first substance may have caused.

The most interesting aspect of all this is that Stan Gutenberg should be fully aware of all the ramifications that I just spelled out. He was a student of ours. We stress those factors repeatedly during their training. I remember him as being fairly bright, asking a lot of questions."

Dr. Hanft commented about the quantity of Valium which had remained in the deceased's stomach, largely undigested, at the time of her death, indicating that she apparently had taken her afternoon medication prior to going to the doctor's office. The blood showed a more than normal amount of pentothal and amytal. More than should be used for psychiatric therapy.

"Well, what do you think our chances are of convincing a grand jury that Dr. Gutenberg committed a crime?" asked Russ Barber.

"I think your chances are good." said Hanft. "I agree," concurred Peterson, "given the fact that Gutenberg is an educated, trained professional who should have known better."

"Next question, if we can convince the County Attorney to call a Grand Jury into session, will the two of you be willing to testify before it?"

Both replied in the affirmative. Dr. Hanft adding, "I would suggest that you try to execute a search warrant for Gutenberg's file on the deceased. That may help in any grand jury deliberations."

"We are going to have to let the County Attorney's office in on this sometime, and this may be soon enough," said Barber, explaining to the two medical professionals our logic and reasoning for not bringing the County Attorney into this case sooner.

"Why wasn't Gutenberg's violation of a year ago brought to the attention of the State Board?" asked Hanft.

*Eli J. Miletich*

I told him about the intercession at that time by attorney Jim Grebbs on behalf of Gutenberg, and of our departments frustration with the County Attorney's staff decision,

"Do you think that this last act was pay back time?" questioned Hanft.

"We don't know," answered Pat Alexander, "but this might be one way of getting the good doctor to cough up, if that possibility even exists."

We thanked the doctors for all their help and returned to Duluth.

On Monday morning, Inspector Barber called County Attorney Keith Brownell and asked him to assign one of his staff to assist us in preparing a search warrant for certain files of a member of the medical profession in Duluth. "Sure, and what doctor are you going after?" he asked.

"Just send someone over and we"ll explain it all to him, then he can brief you later," said Barber.

Brownell sent Velik Kurac, our favorite, who coincidentally was one of Jim Grebbs best friends, socially and professionally.

"Why in hell haven't we been furnished copies of any of these reports previously?" he demanded, when he sat down and started to read.

"Because it has been none of your damn business until now!" replied Inspector Barber in his polite but forceful way, letting Kurac know who was in charge. "This case may have some serious implications, and we did not want anybody on your staff to make a slip of the tongue and screw it up."

"Does Jim Grebbs know that you guys have been conducting this investigation into his wife's death?"

"Hell no, we don't know how he would react toward the doctor," I lied, not revealing what we actually thought about the doctor/ lawyer relationship.

Kurac prepared the application and affidavit for the search warrant as well as the search warrant itself, according to the information we provided him. We, Inspector Barber, Pat Alexander and I, reviewed and scrutinized the final product carefully looking for any deliberate flaw on the part of the preparer. Finding none, Inspector Barber called one of the District Court judges and made arrangements for Pat and me to

39

go to his chambers whereupon the judge read and signed his approval for a search of Dr. Gutenberg's files on Shirley Grebbs.

We took the search party we had put together previously and drove in a hurry to the Medical Arts Building on West Superior Street.

Taking the elevator to the third floor, we walked into the doctor's reception room where the receptionist was a bit shocked to see five plainclothes officers at her desk asking for the doctor.

She stammered, "He is in with a patient, can you wait?"

"Is the patient sedated in any way?" I asked, making sure that we wouldn't be asking the doctor to leave a patient who was out of it.

"No, this is a new patient, and he is only interviewing her."

"Then, we need to see him right now," I stressed.

She walked down the hall, knocked on a door and the doctor appeared, listened to her, then walked down the hall toward us. He did not seem the least bit surprised or irritated.

I read the search warrant to him in its entirety.

He said, "I will show you the file cabinet in which my patients files are kept, but there is no file for Shirley Grebbs. When a patient is deceased, we shred their files. I'm awful sorry, but that's the way it is."

"Doctor, what about billing the family or the insurance company of the deceased. What do you have for documentation or record of your treatment if there is no file?" asked Sergeant Dan Price, one of our search team members.

"We have never had a problem. Here, I will show you the file cabinets, then I have to get back to my patient."

In the file cabinets which were in a small room to the rear of the receptionists desk, we drew a blank.

Price asked the receptionist if she shredded Shirley Grebbs' file and she replied in the negative. "The doctor apparently did," she said.

Price continued along the same vein, "Are all the files and records of deceased patients destroyed or shredded after their passing?"

"Not that I am aware of."

Can you think of any other patients who have died, say in the last two years, that if you went into the cabinets you can find their records?' Price persisted.

"I know of at least three who have passed away," she said, as she rose from her seat, went to the file cabinets, pulled out two drawers and presented us with three folders, "but please don't look into them, the contents are confidential."

Without opening the files, Price jotted down the names of each patient from the cover of their respective folder. It was noteworthy, also, that the cover of each was stamped with the word "DECEASED".

We also learned at that time that Shirley Grebbs had been referred to Dr. Gutenberg by her estranged husband, Jim?????

A grand jury was summoned that week by County Attorney Brownell with one assistant county attorney, Velik Kurac, having a tough time masking his feelings about the whole thing. Of course, we couldn't forget that the doctor almost appeared to know that we were coming with a search warrant. And, wasn't the file on Shirley Grebbs shredded?

Testifying before the grand jury were Pat Alexander, Russ Barber, Dan Price, Dr.'s Hanft and Peterson, and me.

Dr. Gutenberg was indicted for manslaughter.

At his first hearing his attorney, a slick operator from Minneapolis named Sparrow, requested a change of venue without a challenge from Assistant County Attorney Kurac who was representing the prosecution. The change of venue was granted and trial was set for a district court in Minneapolis.

At trial, witnesses were sequestered, meaning that they were not allowed in the courtroom until it was their turn to testify.

Pat Alexander testified, I testified, Dr. Hanft testified and then Dr. Peterson completed the prosecutions case. The State rested.

The words "The State rests," were no sooner our of Kurac's mouth, when defense attorney Sparrow stood and said, "Your honor, the defense asks for a dismissal ruling."

"On what grounds?" asked the judge.

It appeared that defense attorney Sparrow was having a hard time concealing a smirk when he replied, "On the grounds

*Eli J. Miletich*

that the State has failed to establish where this alleged offense took place, and the court fully recognizes that none of the witnesses testified as to where this offense allegedly occurred."

Assistant County Attorney Kurac said not a word.

"You are correct, case dismissed," ruled the judge.

As every lawyer, and most experienced police officers know, at trial the prosecuting attorney must have at least one of his witnesses state, in response to a direct question, the location of the alleged crime, in other words, the city, county and state. That is called establishing jurisdiction.

Our esteemed prosecutor, Velik Kurac, failed to establish jurisdiction!

I was sitting about two pews, rows, back of the attorneys' table in the courtroom and I immediately left my seat, ran up to Velik Kurac and said, "You're going to challenge that aren't you. Put one of us back on the stand, ask us the necessary questions to establish jurisdiction."

"You heard the judges ruling, didn't you?" he snarled through clenched teeth. "You had a shitty case to start with, and there is no appeal either. In the courtroom I hold sway, so go fuck yourself."

I had to control my urge to punch his nose right in the courtroom.

Dr.'s Hanft and Peterson were stunned and we were pissed. After a brief conversation with both, they went on their way, confused at best. Now we clearly understood the lack of challenge to the motion for change of venue.

I called Inspector Russ Barber from a pay phone in the courthouse lobby.

"How's it going?" he asked.

"We're all done, it's dismissed." I said, and followed up by explaining what had happened. "Looks like Velik Kurac got what he wanted all along, he just needed change of venue to pull it off without any local media attention."

"He'll get his reward in hell," said Barber.

The Medical Board of Professional Conduct, having had notice of the doctor's pending trial had contacted our department and our reports were made available to their investigators. Some salvation can be realized by the fact that

45

they held a hearing, and concluded by ruling that Dr. Gutenberg was to have his license immediately and permanently terminated, never allowed to practice psychiatry for the rest of his life.

We should have had at least one, possibly two, convictions, but we will never know.

Velik Kurac, digressed as a prosecutor and became more and more than an occasional drinker and conniver and was ultimately fired by his boss, but not before he became involved in another questionable episode which I'll get to later.

———————————————

Months later, Kurac and another guy, a local defense attorney, former prosecutor himself, tried a not too subtle move to discredit me during a very minor case of felony burglary and marijuana possession.

The former prosecutor, let's call him Pijan, a brilliant attorney who developed a drinking problem when serving in the county attorneys office was no friend of mine. A year or so earlier we had arrested a character for auto theft, on a federal charge, and in his defense arguments in the judge's chambers,

46

he made some disparaging, possibly defamatory, comments about me as it related to my brother, Nick, who every cop, lawyer and judge was well acquainted with. This I heard from Assistant City Attorney Bryan Brown who was in that meeting in Judge McNulty's office. But that's another story.

Carried away by his success in prosecuting several high profile headline homicide cases, during his stint in the County Attorneys office, he had got caught up in the many social congratulatory drinking sessions at Mr. Pete's, a downtown lawyers watering hole. He left the employ of the County to go into private practice apparently thinking that clients would come banging on his door and he would achieve riches.

It doesn't usually turn out that way in a market already flooded with attorneys. It's nice to be on a staff of prosecutors where the overhead costs are borne by the taxpayer and to have a good paycheck coming in every two weeks. To be on your own means necessary overhead expenses such as rent, office staff, telephone, electricity, miscellaneous equipment and so on.

*Eli J. Miletich*

Soon he started to represent some of the very kind of person that he had formerly prosecuted. In jest, I have often said that a silent part of any lawyers solemn oath is that they "must make money by whatever means you can, while you can, ' cause it's a rough world out there."

The Paul Bunyan Bar, another watering hole frequented by bookies, dopers, burglars and other shady characters, became one of his hangouts and you could see the effect his habits and social environment were having on his physical being. From a relatively slender, upright posture and a neat dresser, to a paunchy, sloop shouldered, droopy trousers slob.

Once, based on probable cause, we obtained a search warrant for a suspected marijuana dealers apartment. An informant had made several buys from the suspect, a young male about twenty one years old and, on his last visit to the apartment, the dealer had boasted about how he and a partner had crawled into an unlocked first floor window of the City Clerk's office in City Hall and rummaged through a storage room near the elevator on fourth floor. The confederate of the dealer was an employee at City Hall who was working as a

48

custodian under one of the federal make work programs in existence at that time, and had had the opportunity to unlatch the window before punching out for the day.

They had taken, among other items, a huge, twelve feet by twenty feet, American flag, the one that flies in the Civic Center during the day, and a bronze plaque, dated 1926 or 1927. According to the informant the plaque contained a short phrase of commemoration to the police department on the face and described it as being about the dimension of the cover of a shoe box.

Thus, in addition to the drugs outlined in our application for a search warrant, we named the flag and plaque as items to be searched for and seized, if found.

The search was executed at the residence at 624 East 5th Street. The suspected dealer was not home, but a friend who had crashed the previous night was just waking up. It was about noon. We knocked and he admitted us. I read him the search warrant in the absence of the suspect, and our group fanned out into the various rooms.

*Eli J. Miletich*

Almost immediately one of our guys hollered, "Eli, you've got to see this!" from one of the bedrooms.

Walking in, I was impressed by the bedspread covering the queen size bed, the American flag. It was folded by that officer and placed in a large evidence bag.

"Now let's see if we can find the marijuana and that plaque or whatever it is." I said

Quantities of marijuana were being found in various hiding places in the bedrooms, the living room and the kitchen, i.e., drawers, cabinets, cubby holes, etc.

About an hour and one half later, when we felt we had done a thorough search, we inventoried whatever we had seized on a report and left a copy of that and a copy of the search warrant with the suspected dealers friend and asked him to give it to him when he returned. I also advised him to tell the suspect that we would be requesting an arrest warrant for him. We never did find the plaque.

Based on our reports and the evidence gathered in the search, a warrant for the arrest of the dealer was issued by the court for possession of controlled substances and possession of stolen property. He was later arrested and a trial date set.

The defense attorney was none other than the former prosecutor now one of the favorites of the bad guys. Pijan.

At trial three other officers proceeded to the witness stand before me and gave testimony in response to the prosecutors questions with little or no cross examination by the defense, Pijan.

At noon the judge, C. Luther Eckman, announced a recess for lunch and when the trial resumed there was a noticeable change in the demeanor of our prosecutor who, in case I forgot to mention, was none other than Velik Kurac. His tie was loose and when talking with us prior to going back into the courtroom, we noticed that he smelled of booze. Oh, oh, must have been drinking his lunch at the Whaleback Room of the Radisson Hotel again.

I was the next prosecution witness and explained that the informant, an associate of the defendants burglary partner, had provided information leading to the search warrant which was read, approved and signed by the very same trial judge, C.

Luther Eckman. I related details of how the search turned up various pieces of evidence found by members of the search team.

Cross examination time!

I was grilled, not about the drugs, but about the bronze plaque.

"What size did you say that plaque was, Sergeant Miletich?" Questioned Pijan.

I answered, "The confidential informant described it as about the dimensions of the cover of a shoe box."

"What was the date on the plaque, *SERGEANT* Miletich?" He asked, emphasizing my rank.

"The informant told us it was either 1926 or 1927."

"What did you say was inscribed on the plaque, *SERGEANT* Miletich?"

"The confidential informant was not sure, only that it said something about the Police Department."

Those same questions, in one form or another, were asked repeatedly without any objection from the prosecutor, Kurac, and when I would look in his direction to see what he was up to, his head was tilted upward as if he were counting ceiling tiles, only his eyes were shut.

"Are you sure there was even a plaque at that apartment, *SERGEANT* Miletich?"

I responded, "I can only tell you what information we obtained from the informant and that was included in the search warrant application."

"Did you really have informant information about a plaque?"

"Yes, sir!"

"Isn't it true that there never was a plaque mentioned?"

No objection by prosecutor Kurac.

"That's not correct, there was a plaque mentioned to me and the other officers who interviewed the informant."

"Isn't it true that the plaque business was included in the search warrant application as a guise to allow you and your fellow officers to search every nook and cranny, thus giving you an extension of the right to search and that's how your officers were able to locate evidence which was not in plain sight?"

At that time I looked at Judge Eckman, who also had been looking at Kurac, and asked if we could take a short recess so I could go the the men's room. I had been on the witness stand over an hour and one half but didn't really need to use the john. The judge took a recess.

On the way down from the stand, I stopped at the prosecutors table, looked into Kurac's bleary eyes, bent over and whispered in his ear, "Look, you drunken asshole, if you don't start doing your job, objecting when he's being repetitious and badgering, inferring that I'm lying, I'm going to come down off the stand and knock your chair over to wake you up. It may cost me some time off, But I'm not going to let you set me up because you've got a hard on for me over the Grebbs case, which you threw."

He got wide eyed and looked over at Pijan.

I straightened up and walked out of the courtroom and down the hall to the men's room. I washed my hands and then returned to the courtroom and took the stand again. Velik Kurac was sitting upright.

Pijan started again with the questions he had repeatedly asked before the potty break and to which I had answered, only this time Kurac entered objections which Judge Eckman quickly sustained.

Pijan, now frustrated, wrapped up his cross examination in about five minutes.

The Jury found the defendant guilty on both counts.

At lunch one day, months later, Judge Eckman confided to me that he was about to chastise Kurac just before I asked for a recess. He wondered what I had said to him.

Another episode of a cop doing battle with unscrupulous lawyers in Duluth.

Chapter Four

Duluth is a mid sized city on the southwestern tip of Lake Superior, which, at 32,483 square miles, is the largest of the five Great Lakes, as well as the largest freshwater lake in the world. With those lakes connected to the Atlantic Ocean by the St. Lawrence Seaway, Duluth is 2300 miles from the ocean.

As the western terminus of the Great Lakes-St. Lawrence Seaway System, Duluth has docks which attract vessels from around the world, exporting in gargantuan quantities, iron ore for the steel mills of the lower lakes, mined in the mineral rich Iron Range of northeastern Minnesota. Grain from the fields of the Dakota's, Montana, and Minnesota itself is shipped to eastern ports as well as Europe, Africa and Asia.

Imports include shiploads of steel and fabricated steel products, never sitting well with this city, and region, which has a strong reliance on jobs related to domestic steel production due to its mining and shipping activities.

Duluths population has stabilized at around 87,000 after several recessions since World War II and a population shift to smaller communities outside the city, coupled with the loss of some small manufacturing plants, and the lure, to some, of greener pastures , and deserts of California and other points south and west. It had been at about 105,000 in the early 1950's. The city is twenty eight miles long and about eight miles at the widest part.

Minnesota Mining and Manufacturing, known in recent years as the 3M Corporation, had its beginnings on the north shore of Lake Superior, making sandpaper from the fine sand found on the beaches of the lake.

With most of the downtown situated on a steep hill overlooking part of the lake, and one of its main tributaries, the St. Louis River, Duluth is often compared to its larger cousin on the West Coast, San Francisco.

Originally occupied by the Sioux and Chippewa (nee:Ojibwa) tribes of the western lakes, the land was mainly settled by the Chippewa when the first Europeans were known to have visited this area, French explorers and fur traders, came in the late 1600's. The Chippewa had made war on the Sioux and banished them to the Dakota's upon their defeat.

An early visitor was an adventurer-explorer-fur trader, in 1689, Daniel Greysolon, Sir du Lhut, a member of French nobility. Hence the city's name. French voyageurs and trappers, then the English, operated trading posts in the region for over a century and one quarter until treaties with the tribes opened the lands for permanent settlement in the 1840's. Many small communities sprung up in the area, most linked to fur trading and the early harvesting of lumber from virgin forests.

When large deposits of iron ore were discovered in the wilderness to the north of Duluth in the 1870's, a boom town akin to that of western gold mining towns was the atmosphere in the new developing port. Lumber, in abundance became an even bigger prize and a great number of mining and timber barons suddenly cropped up with eastern ties. The J.P. Morgans, the James Hill and the Rockefellers, even a local, Chester Congdon, were names bandied about as those who were gobbling up all the valued and prosperous land.

Seven explorer brothers, the Merritt's, later dubbed the "Seven Iron Men of the North," were discoverers of the largest iron ore fields, many of which are being mined yet. They worked those mines and built a railroad to carry the ore to the Port of Duluth. Borrowing money from those eastern magnates, the Merritts soon became their prey and then victims. Precious land grabbed from the Merritt's became a foundation for what was to become the giant conglomerate U.S. Steel Corporation.

When the city was incorporated in 1858 law enforcement rested with a 'vigilance' committee. Its' first police chief was appointed in April, 1870. He was a rough hewn gentleman named Robert S. Bruce. Since he was one of the toughest men in this thriving, bustling new port town, and the fact that he was the head of law enforcement as it existed, one of his chores was to take the revenue from the City Treasurer's office to the city's only bank for deposit.

On a warm summer day in the last week of June, 1870, the Mayor, who also doubled as City Treasurer, called on Bruce to make delivery of funds, said to be around nine thousand dollars, to the bank.

The Chief dutifully received the courier bag, left City hall for the bank and was never to be seen or heard from again. He had been Chief for six weeks.

59

*Eli J. Miletich*

Theories as to Chief Bruce's fate ranged from outright enterprising theft and relocation to a faraway place, to his being set upon by some of the local toughs of that time, relieved of his burden, then dumped into the cold waters of Lake Superior, tied to one of the many large boulders which grace the lakes shores. We'll never know, but I subscribe to the latter theory, giving the guy the benefit of doubt.

History and science have shown that from the numerous accidental drownings on the big lake, very few bodies have been recovered. Dr. Julius Wolff, a professor at the University of Minnesota, Duluth, an expert on the facts and mysteries of Lake Superior, as well as other scientists, insists that the many stratum, i.e., layers of water, each at radically differing temperatures, prevents a submerged body from penetrating the next layer above. Lake Superior does not give up her dead.

In any event, in the 1870's, $9,000 was nothing to sneeze at.

## October 1

"Who?" said a police dispatcher in Boulder, Colorado.

"Sergeant Pat Alexander, Duluth, Minnesota Police Department." Replied Alexander to the voice on the other end of the long distance call he had placed to the Boulder Police Department.

"What in the hell is a daloot?" was the cute reply.

Alexander, not wanting to get into it with an agency he was calling for information and perhaps, cooperation, calmly gave a geography lesson to the dispatcher and requested to speak to a supervisor or an investigator. He was transferred to a uniform division sergeant.

"Who?"

"Not again," thought Alexander, resisting the temptation to tell the guy to go to hell. After the same amenities, he explained that a battered, unidentified womans' body had been found in Duluth with only the matchbook from a bar in Boulder found in her slacks pocket.

"So what, she could've been visiting Colorado, couldn't she?" came the unsympathetic response, "People pick up matchbooks when they stop somewhere for a drink or a cup of coffee or even when they gas up their car, you know."

"Sergeant, could I have your name?" said Alexander, "We know we're looking at a long shot, but if you could be a little more cooperative, we could get on with our investigation and not be a big bother to you any longer than necessary."

Taken back a bit, the Boulder cop said, "My name is Shotley and I'm a Sergeant assigned to a supervisory position in the street patrol division. Just what is it you would like from us?"

Boulder is a city of some seventy seven thousand people in the Denver metropolitan area, and it has a crime rate attendant to big city living which might explain the blase' response of Shotley, but his initial attitude was uncommon between police officers when help was requested. Matter of fact, it didn't improve much, other than the the noticeable curbing of his smart ass comments.

"The matchbook has Tropicana Lounge printed on it, with a phone number, 556-8724." said Alexander, "Is it possible that you could have a patrol unit stop at that place to check if anyone there is familiar with our victim?"

"We could try, but don't get your hopes up, that place was a real classy joint back in the fifties and early sixties, but it kind of went down hill and now it features punk rock and is always crowded with bikers and the like. It is a trouble spot, lots of tourists looking for a little excitement."

"Yes," said Alexander, "could you run a check of missing persons in your city and area? The victim is in her mid twenties, olive complected, five feet two inches tall, about one hundred two pounds, with short black hair, possibly of mid east ancestry."

"If by Mid East you mean Egyptian or one of those Arab countries, we've got thousands of 'em living here since the Iranian revolution, Pakistan and Afghans too. They're a closed mouth bunch. Lot's of luck."

"I realize the effort I'm asking of you folks, but we'd do the same for you if it were the other way around, and I do appreciate your help. Can you call me back one way or the other? My number is 218-723-2332, thanks and have a good

63

day," said Alexander, closing off the conversation, but he did have some question about the professionalism of Boulder's police.

Alexander then called Inspector Fred Sowl, briefed him as to his conversation with Shotley and the autopsy findings.

Sowl passed the same info on to me with the comment that he "thought Pat was digging right in, and if anyone was going to come up with something, right now, I'm comfortable that he and the guys assisting him will."

I smiled at Fred's comments.

I still felt strongly about our investigators not allowing any possible clue or evidence to be overlooked and thought back to a double homicide, eleven years earlier, in one of Minnesota's largest mansions, belonging to one of the states wealthiest families.

The Congdon Mansion is located on a 7.6 acre plot of land about twenty blocks northeast of downtown Duluth on the shore of Lake Superior.

Millionaire Chester Congdon built this home to use as his primary residence and focal point for his thriving iron mining business. The majority of his vast holdings was in iron ore, but he was known in eastern seaboard financial circles as a timber and iron baron. That was polite. Many of the explorers and adventurers who had ventured into the wilds of Minnesota and who had lost their claims to Congdon and others of his ilk, such as the Morgans, the Rockefellers, the Hills and other corporate giants, would refer to them as the robber barons.

One would only need to get into a conversation with a descendant of one of the Seven Iron Men of Minnesota, the Merritt brothers, to hear how they discovered huge iron ore deposits, started mining and building a railroad to haul the mineral to the port of Duluth only to lose their rights to unscrupulous "financiers." But, that is another story.

The mansion was started in 1905 with the finest and most exquisite materials used in its construction. Lumber from South America, marble from Greece, gas lights from Germany. Completed in 1908 at a then estimated cost of around $865,000, some say that it is very likely one of the most beautiful homes of its kind ever built in the United States.

About two years after the homicides, the heirs to the estate turned the mansion and property over to the University of Minnesota and it presently serves as a historical landmark open to the public, for a fee of course.

Chester and his wife, Clara, moved into the mansion after it was completed and lived comfortably with their seven children and it remained in the family for almost seventy years.

Virtually all the children found their way away from the roost, building or buying other homes, with one of the daughters, young Elizabeth, given title to the estate. She was deeply involved in Duluth's community, especially in what nice folks would refer to as society, sponsoring scores of local programs and activities.

Elizabeth Congdon was in her eighties in 1977 and the last surviving child of Chester and Clara.

That Chester had built his fortune by shrewd takeovers and investments in mining and timber was well known, and he was catered to and feared, especially by politicians in the city as well as in St. Louis County.

Quite infirmed, Elizabeth had spent the last twenty odd years of her life under twenty four hour care of professional nurses, traveling to the other family estate, in Arizona, for five winter months, taking several of the nurses with her. In fact, the wife of one of my sergeants, Gene Ethan, was a registered nurse who was so employed back in the fifties and sixties.

A spinster, Elizabeth had adopted two toddler girls years back, raising them to adulthood as members of that wealthy family, then seeing them depart the nest as most children are prone to do.

One adopted daughter, content with a modest trust established for her, completed college, met an energetic professional man, married and settled down to raise a family.

The other girl, Marjorie, took advantage of every opportunity to get as much as the old lady would allow her, hitting her up for money long after she had left the household, supposedly to build and establish her own life.

Marjorie started her post secondary education at an elite, fashionable women's college out east, but never quite finished, drifting around the country, calling her mother for additional money whenever her trust allotment for the year had been exhausted. Elizabeth always came through.

In her early twenties Marjorie met and married a man in Colorado named Richard LeRoy, and after two children, they divorced. Marjorie resumed her drifting, but returned to Colorado occasionally.

In 1975, after her divorce from LeRoy was final, Marjorie moved back to Colorado with her son, settling in the town of Golden where she met her future husband, Roger Caldwell. They were married in 1976 by a justice of the peace and right away found themselves knee deep in money problems. Both were spendthrifts, but Marjorie did have some income from the trust set up by adopted mom Elizabeth. They proceeded to draw out cash with no care or concern as to whether or not the well would ever run dry.

Elizabeth, not pleased with the course of Marjorie's life, was even more dismayed when she met Roger and had an opportunity to study him. A gold digging fortune hunting S.O.B. is the way she described him, in confidence, to several close relatives.

The Caldwell's had decided that Colorado was the place they wanted to live and found some ranch land southwest of Denver, signing contracts for $750,000 for purchase of the property.

That acquisition was ill fated as Marjorie had depleted most of the money in trust, her half of one million. Marjorie truly loved horses, buying and selling dozens in the months that followed their move to ranching. Bad deals in that regard and other immature spending soon showed up in deficit bank statements.

The bank started the process for repossession and foreclosure of the entire ranch. They were desperate, but knew exactly to whom they should appeal.

*Eli J. Miletich*

Roger Caldwell made a trip to Duluth in the spring of 1977 to meet with mother Elizabeth and her financial trustees. Marjorie was first in line to inherit a major segment of the entire estate, as she was the oldest of Elizabeth's two adopted daughters, though the money and property were not quite hers as Elizabeth, in her eighties and not in the best of health, looked like she might go on for several years yet. Roger asked the trustees for $800,000 which would enable paying off the bank. Elizabeth turned him down.

Shortly after returning to Colorado he met with another member of the Congdon family in Denver to hit him up for the money. He was turned down again.

The Caldwell's could not find a way to come up with the needed money. The repossession clock was ticking.

On the last weekend of June, 1977, Elizabeth had spent a few days at her summer home on the Brule River in northern Wisconsin and, upon returning on the evening of the 26th, being very tired from traveling, she went right to her room to rest. Her nurse, Velma Pietala, helped her to bed just a few minutes before eleven P.M. Mrs. Pietala was one of the crew of

70

nurses providing her round the clock care. Ironically, Mrs. Pietala had retired in May of that year, but had agreed to fill in for one of the other nurses who was on vacation.

Early on the morning of the 27th, the day nurse, reporting for work at the mansion prior to, as usual, the rest of the household staffs' arrival from nearby quarters on the estate, admitted herself with a key, but was puzzled at not being greeted in the foyer by the night nurse, Pietala. She was carrying her umbrella, fearing it was going to rain as it had for so many days the past month.

Placing her umbrella in the stand near the main door, she proceeded through the reception room and walked up the stairway leading to the second floor where Elizabeth Congdon's bedroom was located. As she approached the landing midway between the floors and was about to make a turn to the left, she noticed the legs, then saw Velma Pietala's body sprawled out on the next flight of stairs.

Her head was battered almost beyond recognition and there was blood splattered all about. She checked for a pulse and

*Eli J. Miletich*

found none, then quickly walked the remaining stairs to Elizabeth's room.

As she entered the room everything appeared in place, except for the pillow covering Miss Congdon's head.

Removing the pillow, she saw the staring eyes of death.

She quickly called the police from the phone on the night stand near the bed and, after that, one of the Congdon relatives from the maternal side of the family.

The call came into the Duluth Police Department just shortly after Detective Sergeant Richard Yagoda had reported for work and the desk officer had buzzed him back in the Detective Bureau. As Sergeant Ross Browne was walking in the Bureau door, Yagoda grabbed him and said, "Come with me."

"What's up, Dick?"

"There's two dead bodies at the Congdon Mansion."

When they arrived they found a very distraught day nurse, June Pogled, who kept repeating, "It was them, it was them."

When pressed by Yagoda as to whom was "them?", she said, 'Talk to Miss Congdon's nephew, Everett, he will tell you." Adding, "Velma's car is gone too!"

A cursory check of the mansion revealed that a window in a walkout door at the basement level had been broken, indicating that this may have been the point of entry by the intruder, or intruders, if there were more than one.

A bloodied brass candelabra was found at the top of the stairs near Elizabeth's room.

Browne quickly found a phone and called police headquarters for the office of Ray Pound, Inspector of Detectives, his boss.

"Ray, this is Ross, we've got a big one out here at the Congdon Mansion. The old lady has been suffocated in her bed with a pillow and her night nurse is dead, head smashed with a brass candelabra. I think you should come out here yourself."

"Any press of media there yet, Ross?" asked Pound. "No," replied Browne.

"Good, no comments until I get there," directed Pound, "You can brief me and show me the layout of the crime scene and the mansion itself. I want to have some answers when they come. Be sure to tell Yagoda that I will be the only one talking to the press on this case."

*Eli J. Miletich*

Both individuals, Browne and Pound, claimed to detest politicians and asserted themselves to be apolitical, but here was a classic instance of politics about to be played out.

Wasn't it Shakespeare who wrote, "Me thinks thou protest thine innocence much too loudly."

When he arrived at the estate, which now had uniformed police officers at the gates by the previous direction of Yagoda, Pound was accompanied by Sergeant Perry Zid, who had only recently been promoted to Detective Sergeant from a long time assignment as an ID Tech. That previous position had provided Zid, a bright young cop, an opportunity to show his qualities and he developed into a very skilled crime scene investigator, impulsive and imperious, yet skilled.

Because he was one of Pound's favorites, Zid's assignment to the ID Bureau came about after slightly more than two years on the job, much to the dismay of veteran officers.

As a protege of Pound, he was also more or less immune from criticism, and heaven help the career of anyone who questioned the work of Perry Zid. All in all, his good work soon

74

overcame whatever petty, but deserved, jealousy which may have been generated.

Another ID Tech had also been told to respond to the scene and was a couple minutes behind the Inspector on arrival. It was officer Terry Rivers.

----

Duluth's crime scene officers are called Identification Technicians or ID Officers. The title differs from police department to police department but essentially intelligent, eager, hard working young patrolman are appointed to this generally prestigious, important position. Rivers fit the description in virtually all areas with respect to work performance.

Here was a guy who, whenever his wife had her monthly discomfort, took at least one, sometimes two days, off for 'Sickness in the Family', a clause in the union contract with the City. His boss had spoken with him on several occasions to no avail. Naturally, these days off were with pay, thus paid for by the taxpayers. It was intended to be a needed benefit for employees. Abuse of this feature was not meant or desired to

75

be tolerated by the employer or employees. When an individual was off for such a reason, there was no replacement, thus units would be obligated to operate short handed, and in police work that can be hazardous.

As Police Union President some dozen years earlier, I had led negotiations which brought this feature into reality, and Rivers was stretching the point, to put it mildly.

Once, when the repeated offense had been brought to my attention by the Services Division head, Inspector Walt Peterson, with documentation showing his use of Sickness in the Family coinciding with his wife being off sick, he asked that Rivers be brought in for a discussion and review of his and his family's health. I approved, but told Walt, "This is going to be brief. Line it up and have Deputy Chief Sisto come in for the meeting also."

I had been appointed Police Chief five and one half years earlier and, as is common in virtually all law enforcement agencies, a hard core group remained who, because their favorite did not 'make it', attempted to usurp, disrupt or be just plain assholes whenever the opportunity arose. The Duluth Police Department is no exception.

How's the family?" I asked.

"Fine sir."

"Kids all healthy?" I followed up.

"Sure, they're living with their mother, my first wife, but they're doing fine." Said Rivers.

"How about the wife, how's she doing?"

"My first wife I never see, except when I go to pick up the kids," Rivers said, "But my present wife is in good health, and is going great since she started working nearby in an office in City Hall. We ride to work together when I'm on the day shift."

"Then, to get to the point, please explain to the Inspector, the Deputy Chief and me, just why you feel justified in the use of twenty seven days of sick leave last year, fourteen of which were for sickness in the family," I said with emphasis, "Likewise, twenty four days the year before, and in the first five months of this year, you already have fifteen days racked up?"

"Well, the contract—."

"Don't give me any bullshit about the contract," I cut him off, "I've been the major contributor to the makeup of that document since the first written one was drawn up in 1971, and I know that feature is intended for use in the case of real sickness of an employee's dependent wife or child if there was no other assistance available. Thus, it enables the employee to attend to that family member until help can be arranged for or to take that person to a doctor or hospital, but in no event for any period longer than one day, but not for reasons we suspect to be invalid. A wife's monthly discomfort is sure as hell an invalid reason for an employee to be off 'Sickness in the Family'.

"Well, Chief, that's how it is, when my wife is feeling poorly, I'm going to stay home to care for her." Claimed Rivers.

"Like hell it is!" I said. "Let me tell you that the department views that attitude as irresponsible, and in fact, you are screwing the taxpayers, and that amounts to fraud, so listen closely," I emphasized again, "Your use of sick leave for whatever purported reason is going to be monitored and whenever you choose to call in sick, or sickness in the family, you had better have the coffee pot on, because there is going to be a supervisor at your front door before you hang up the phone. They will make a determination as to whether or not you are pulling a con job, and if so, will see that an immediate appointment is made for a visit to your doctor or an emergency room, if necessary. That applies to your wife, in that she is also a city employee. If the decision is that you're full of shit, disciplinary action will follow. Am I clear?"

"Yes sir," was the terse reply from an obviously perturbed Rivers.

"Then return to your assigned duties and don't let this kind of problem with you be brought to our attention again," I concluded, standing up from behind my desk, signifying that the session was over.

"Whew, is he pissed," said Walt Peterson, Rivers' bureau boss, "he was so white, I thought he was going to faint. We'll have to wait and see if this did any good."

"I know one thing," I said, "we've made enemies of him and his wife today, or should I say, I've made enemies?"

Time will tell, I mused.

*Eli J. Miletich*

## Chapter Seven

A quick conference with Yagoda and Browne told Pound all he needed to know for the time being; the basement door with a smashed window appeared to be the point of entry. Nurse Pietala had apparently heard the intruder from her room across from Elizabeth's and surprised him or her on the stairway where he/she struck the nurse repeatedly with a candelabra taken from a pedestal situated at the mid point landing on the stairway. Cuts and abrasions on her hands and forearms were an indication that she had tried to fend off the blows.

The bloody weapon was found at the top of the stairs where the assailant had apparently dropped it.

There were no suspects at this point although Pound was curious about the statement that nurse Pogled had blurted out to Yagoda. "It was them." Adding, "Talk to Miss Congdon's nephew, Everett Vann, he will tell you."

Pound shortly learned that the nephew, Vann, was at the main gate to the estate and he gave word to allow him to pass. "We need to talk with him." He told Zid.

An engineer, Vann was a professional to the bone. A graduate of one of the nations military academies, he was commissioned a lieutenant and assigned to Korea during that 'police action', commanding an engineer battalion which was responsible for bridge building, housing, fortifications and other construction needs, however, his men also were equipped with the weapons of war, and they used them. The outfit earned many citations.

Upon discharge from the army, Vann formed his own engineering and architectural firm without any of the family money and was now a community leader in his own right. He did retain an interest in the military, continuing with a reserve unit.

After hearing of the circumstances of the death of this aunt and her nurse, Vann pondered a moment and said, "It could have been Marjorie and Roger."

"Who are they?" asked Pound.

"Marjorie is one of my aunts adopted daughters, and Roger Caldwell is her present husband. She has been bleeding

*Eli J. Miletich*

Elizabeth for money for the past ten years, always with a phony story of an emergency of one kind or another."

"Where do they live?" asked Pound.

"Outside Denver about thirty miles or so."

"Have they been to Duluth lately?" Pound continued with the interview.

"Around the last week in May, Roger was at Elizabeth's and was pressing her for about eight hundred thousand dollars, or they allegedly were going to lose their ranch in Colorado.

Elizabeth refused and told him that he and Marjorie needed to straighten out their lives or Marjorie may in fact be cut off in her will."

"How do you know this?" Pound asked.

"Elizabeth called me after Roger left and told me about that visit as well as the many other times she had given Marjorie money," said Vann, adding, "She also told me that Roger was very disturbed when he left and she felt that he might do something foolish. I was thinking that this meant something like torching the ranch for insurance, but not this."

"Let's see, it's Monday today, do you know if either Marjorie or Roger, or both, might have been town this past weekend?"

"I doubt it," replied Vann, "Elizabeth assured me in May that if they ever showed up again, she would have one of the household staff contact me immediately."

With that, Vann left to contact a mortuary and make other arrangements.

Pound huddled again with Browne, Yagoda and Zid. Yagoda suggested calling the department and having one of the early reporting Day Shift detectives go to the Duluth International Airport to check the flight manifest, i.e., passenger list, for any flights which had left directly for Denver or for a stopover in the Twin Cities, which may have allowed for the suspect to make his way to Denver. It was 7:56 A.M.

At police headquarters, I was back in the Narco office and took a call from the desk officer. "Got anybody back there with you yet, Sergeant?" He asked.

"Not yet, but I'm expecting Denny Lepak any minute now, we've got some state Crime Bureau guys coming in town who we're going to set up with an informant to make some

83

controlled buys from a dealer we've been after for a while. Why do you ask?"

He quickly told me about the double homicide at the Congdon mansion and as he did so, Lepak walked into the office. The desk officer gave me basic details and said that they needed someone to check out flights at the airport, and since no one was in the Detective Bureau, could we run out there?

I told Lepak of the murders and we left word for the other members of our unit, who were due any time, to meet with the state agents. We were on our way. En route, I briefed Lepak about the possible suspects, Marjorie and Roger Caldwell, and that we were to check on the possibility of them traveling out of Duluth by commercial airlines.

"What if they were traveling under assumed, phony, names?" Denny asked. "We'll pay hell in trying to figure out from passenger lists who they might be, especially if they didn't book their seats together. And, where is it they are believed to be living?"

"Outside of Denver. We've got to remember to have the people at Republic Airlines provide us with the passenger

84

manifests for flights out of Minneapolis-St. Paul, as well as Duluth, with Denver as the destination."

At the Republic Airlines counter, we were directed to a supervisor, Larry Johnson, who, after we ID'd ourselves and told him the nature of our visit, was very cooperative.

Johnson, a not too uncommon name in Minnesota, said, "Let's see, there was one flight that left from Duluth to Denver, non stop, at 8:00 A.M., that's about twenty three minutes ago."

"How about any flight leaving for the Twin Cities which might have a connecting flight for Denver?" Asked Denny.

"There was a Twin Cities flight that left here at 6:55 A.M., over an hour and one half ago, with a connecting flight to Denver at, hmm, let's see, 8:25 A.M." said Johnson.

I asked, "Can we have someone in the Cities check the passengers for our people before that flight takes off?"

"Virtually impossible.

I think the only thing you fellows can hope for now is to check the flight manifest for all these flights and maybe your suspects names will show up." Said Johnson.

He then went into a computer, pushed a couple buttons and in a half minute we had the passenger lists for the Duluth-Denver flight and the Duluth-Twin Cities as well as the Twin Cities-Denver flights.

No Marjorie Congdon. No Marjorie Caldwell. No Roger Caldwell. Worst of all, no male, female couples traveling together.

"How many tickets were purchased at the counter as against advance purchases?" I asked Larry Johnson.

"Usually, and that's true for today, about ten per cent are at the counter."

"Do your clerks usually request identification from people when they buy tickets at the counter?" I queried.

If it's a regular flyer, no, even if it's by check. All others, if by check, we ask for ID, but if it's cash, no request for ID is made."

"When does that direct flight arrive in Denver?" Pursued Lepak.

"Ten o'clock, A.M., Central Time, you know, Denver is on Mountain Time, so it will be nine in that time zone."

I then questioned about the arrival of the flight from Minneapolis-St. Paul Airport, and he said, "Ten thirty, Central time."

Before leaving the airport, I called Detective Sergeant Dan Price, who when he arrived at work, had been given the assignment of screening all incoming phone calls reference the murders and forwarding messages of importance to Inspector Pound. I briefed him on what we found out at the airport and he suggested that it might be a good idea to contact the Airport Police at Stapleton International Airport in Denver and request that they meet both scheduled Republic arrivals in question for the purpose of manually checking the identification of each deplaning passenger. I agreed.

"But, I think I will pass that thought on to Inspector Pound out at the scene to see what he thinks," added Dan.

By now Pound had designated Zid as the Incident Coordinator with all the other officers in supporting roles. Yagoda, the most experienced, streetwise and skillful of those at the scene, was told, "This is Perry's case and if he needs help or suggestions from you, he'll ask. In the meantime, try to stay out of the way. Ross Browne will be Perry's assistant coordinator."

It was shortly after that dramatic scene was played out that Price called the mansion, spoke to Browne and made the suggestion about calling the Denver Airport Police and requesting their assistance by checking all passengers coming from Minnesota cities for the next several hours.

Browne said, "I'll check with the boss," and put Price on hold for a few minutes.

When they spoke again, Browne said, "Ray is getting ready for a press briefing and Perry says that there is plenty of time to check out that hunch."

"It's not a hunch, asshole," said Dan, "There's a good chance, if Marjorie or her husband, or both, are real suspects, that they may be on one of those flights under phony names, especially since the murders occurred only last night. Think it through, if they did it and now want to get back to their homes to establish an alibi, we ought to rule out that possibility at least. I'm sure that the Denver cops will also be glad to help, and it won't cost a dime. I think we should follow through on this!"

"Well, it's not your case, so butt out," retorted Browne.

In the meantime, Sergeant Perry Zid had instructed ID Tech Rivers, assisting at the mansion with the crime scene technical stuff, to start dusting the entire stairway and the candelabra for prints. As an afterthought, he directed Rivers to include the washrooms of both Elizabeth and nurse Pietala in the event the assailant had used one of the washrooms to clean blood from his/her person. Zid, the former ID Tech, assisted with those efforts.

Interestingly, nurse Velma Pietala's missing vehicle, a Plymouth Fury, was found that afternoon by airport police in the parking ramp at the Minneapolis-St. Paul International Airport, one hundred sixty five miles south of Duluth! "Butt out," the man had said.

## Chapter Eight

When Browne, Zid and Pound finally decided that they should ask Denver cops for help, at around 11:30 A.M., they learned that all planes from Minnesota had arrived. An airport check of deplaning passengers was out of the question, and the Denver PD people who checked at the ranch found Roger Caldwell still in bed, with Marjorie fixing breakfast. It was 11:55 A.M. Mountain Time. It was learned, much later in the case, that Roger had arrived on the flight from the Twin Cities.

A key piece of evidence was a small wicker type basket found in a search of the Caldwell house, which a clerk in a Twin Cities International Airport gift shop remembered selling to a guy who she picked from mug photos. The purchase allegedly took place in the early morning hours of June 27th. The photo picked by the clerk was that of Roger Caldwell. Now, the question begs to be asked: The last time you purchased an item at an airport gift shop, did the clerk even look you in the eye or study your face as she rang up the money you paid?

An interesting side bar to that episode is that during one of the many press briefings over the weeks of the investigation, Pound had made an announcement of an important development.

"The dusting of the crime scene which had been ordered and directed, as well as assisted by Sergeant Perry Zid, had turned up a palm print on the edge of the wash basin in nurse Pietala's washroom. The State Crime Bureau Laboratory is processing the print, hopefully to aid in identifying the assailant."

Nothing was forthcoming about the results of the processing of the print for several weeks.

At one of the press briefings about a month later, an inquisitive reporter asked for an update and a very sheepish Pound reluctantly said, "The lab compared it with possible suspects with negative results."

Pressed further by that reporter, Pound was compelled to add, "However, to exclude everyone who was at the crime scene after the fact, a comparison was made with all officers

91

prints. The print turned out to be that of Detective Sergeant

Perry Zid, and understandable error."

Was such an "error" committed by an experienced crime

scene investigator really "understandable"?

Subsequently, several things, among them, the wicker

basket, a coin believed to be missing from Elizabeth Congdon's

bedroom and found in Roger Caldwell's possession, the gift

shop clerks pick of Roger from the photo line up, and other bits

of circumstantial evidence, led to the indictment of Marjorie

Congdon Caldwell and Roger Caldwell for murder. They were

tried separately with each trial being media circuses captivating

the interest of the whole state.

---

That leads to a bit of background on one of the two men

seeking PR from the case.

Inspector Pound was a study in human character.

Personally and socially he was full of charm and the life of the

party whenever he was around.

He had benefited from the fact that when he started on the

police department in the fifties, the individuals of his Polish ethnic stock had evolved to supervisory roles within the department.

After a short stint in patrol, he was successful in a promotional exam, advanced to Sergeant and assigned to the Traffic Division, Accident Investigation Unit, not because of any exceptional work on his part, but because of the contacts he had established, and by being just a nice guy. He was intelligent, however not one to rock the boat, always displaying a cool, calm and laid back outlook. His work product reflected the same mentality, not going out of his way to resolve anything at hand if it meant he would end up in the middle of it.

After several years, he wrote an excellent exam for lieutenant, finishing number one on the promotional list and when so promoted, assigned directly into the Detective Bureau, Auto Theft Unit, instead of what was then the obligatory tour as a Patrol Lieutenant before even receiving consideration for assignment to the Detective Bureau.

Soon, he and a guy he frequently partnered with started receiving notice, behind their backs, for their particular style of 'shirt pocket investigations'.

*Eli J. Miletich*

On our department most officers, including investigators, have one thing in mind, solve a problem or case, share information and seek assistance from all others who may be able to contribute to that end. Not Pound and his partner.

In any matter which showed the potential for headlines or a lead story on the six o'clock news, they kept all reports in their suit coat chest pocket, not sharing info which possibly could tie in with the work of other officers, nor seeking possible related facts or evidence from them. Thus, the 'shirt pocket' tag.

Case in point, there was a Lakeside neighborhood homicide whereby a woman was bludgeoned with a sharp edged weapon, and they were the lead investigators. Other detectives assigned to assist were able to obtain little in the way of cooperative info and likewise, because of that, shared little.

The primary suspect from the start was the husband. When our two heroes found a steel angle iron, about two feet long, over the rafters in the basement of the victims home; she had been found in the cold of a Minnesota winter night outside their home, clad only in her nightgown, they kept this from the others on the investigative team and naturally created more resentment when they moved for an arrest warrant based on lab report results which showed blood of the victim in small traces on the iron.

The suspect, Jo Hyleck, a prominent insurance agent in the city, was subsequently convicted, served a short term, released because of declining health and died of cancer. His last will and testament decreed that he be cremated and that his ashes dropped from an airplane over the county court house where he was convicted. He even left money to pay for the small aircraft to do the deed, but that wasn't discovered until after the fact. There were some on the department, in a display of sick humor, who said that he also should have willed that some of ashes be dropped over our heroes homes.

As I have pointed out, they never seemed to realize that teamwork is paramount in police work if the public is to be served properly. Unfortunately, they left some heirs to their kind of thinking, and in the years that I was Chief, they were a source of some minor irritation which needed to be addressed from time to time.

---

*Eli J. Miletich*

Several years later, after progressing through the ranks, and now in command of the Detective Bureau, Inspector Pound showed that he was not above some chicanery.

On a Wednesday night, during a Police Welfare Association meeting, he was paged quietly by a member of the Juvenile Bureau and left the hall. Nothing unusual about that.

However, when the meeting ended and many of us passed by the Juvenile Bureau and observed, through the glass door, a small group of department insiders of that period, we sensed that something serious was up. Trying to find out in the next few days was like running up against that proverbial brick wall.

A couple days later a veteran sergeant working in the Uniform Patrol Division abruptly retired. Usually when a guy has plans to retire, at least his immediate co-workers know about it. No one saw him to ask questions about his sudden, unexpected action.

About two, maybe three, weeks later there was a short item in the local news papers court column about an adult male, the former sergeant, pleading guilty in Juvenile Court to the offense, 'Contributing to the Delinquency of a Juvenile'.

96

Under Minnesota law, Juvenile Court proceedings are confidential, thus the public is not privy to the facts of the incident. On our department it's not that easy to keep secrets once a part of the story gets out.

By and large the facts saw daylight, even though by decree of the then Detective Inspector, the entire file was pulled from the Records Bureau, as well as from the Juvenile Bureau. I found that file in a cabinet when I moved into the Chief's office.

The veteran sergeant had been playing around with children of relatives, a simple matter of inter familial sex, and was tripped up when one of his victims went to a social service agency for personal help in dealing with the victims emotions.

The sergeant was allowed to retire, thus preserving his pension, and with the proceedings conducted in Juvenile Court, the identity of the victims, as well as the perpetrator, were preserved. The same privacy of the kids would have been assured in Adult Court but the difference is that details of the sordid crime would have been exposed. It mattered that the sergeant was one of the 'good old boys'.

Asked about it several years later, by me, Pound could only rationalize by saying, "It was the only way to protect the kids".

---

After their indictments for homicide in the Condgon-Pietala case, Roger was tried first and convicted. A couple months later, Marjorie's trial was held in Hastings, Minnesota, one hundred seventy miles south of Duluth. Her attorneys had argued successfully for a change in venue. Marjorie was acquitted.

On appeal, the Minnesota Supreme Court set aside Roger Caldwell's conviction, ordering a new trial.

Plea Bargaining, a nemesis to good, hardworking cops, but professional bliss for lawyers, ensued, and a deal was arrived at whereby Roger pled guilty and was sentenced to time already served, four years. Justice?

Up to the time of his death of cancer several years later in his home state of Pennsylvania, Caldwell continued to maintain innocence, claiming that he only pled guilty to avoid another long, stressful, trial.

That case was handled by persons proclaiming themselves to be apolitical, but who played politics due to misdirected ambitions. However, the press did receive its briefings.

As a great police chief in Los Angeles said about twenty five years ago, "Ambition is a valued trait in a good cop. He or she should aspire to be the best in the profession. A police officer or police chief who say that they disdain politics and politicians should find themselves another career, because the test is whether one can decipher the political motives of the players in the community scene and react to those motives in an honest and positive manner. Only then will the public have been served properly."

Press conferences do not win criminal trials.

---

One more example before we leave the ranch, oops, mansion.

When I was still a sergeant coordinating the efforts of the Narco-Vice Unit, I was also continuing with my elected duties as president of the police union and had been a regional vice president of the International Union of Police Associations as

*Eli J. Miletich*

well as the International's finance committee chair. In that capacity there was a responsibility to convene a two day meeting, in Washington D.C., of members of that committee, comprised of vice presidents from other parts of the country. These meetings were held twice per year to receive a report from the Secretary-Treasurer as well as to do an audit and prepare a report. In as much as this was an official duty on behalf of the International, it required that expenses be provided by that organization. One of the most coincidental, freakish, developments in a criminal case occurred due to my need to cash that expense check and purchase travelers checks.

It was April 13th on a nice spring day in the late 70's and I had walked from police headquarters to the Northern City National Bank in downtown Duluth, about a ten minute walk.

At about 3:20 P.M. I entered the bank and went directly to the tellers window of Joyce intending to get those travelers checks.

Joyce is the wife of an old friend, Scotty McLeod, of Duluth golf fame, a West Duluth guy I have known most of my life, and I usually kid with her when I go to the bank.

There was only one person ahead of me in the line, a white male, approximately nineteen or twenty years old, with moderate length brown hair, having what appeared to be wide bug eyes. I noticed that he smelled of alcohol. At that time in Minnesota's history, one needed to be only nineteen to consume booze.

I overheard him ask Mrs. McLeod if he could cash in some change and she replied, "Yes".

He proceeded to empty his left front trouser pocket of several handfuls of coins, which appeared to be all silver.

Just about that time he noticed me standing to his left rear, I was in civvies, and he stepped aside as if to make room for me. I simply smiled and said that I had to make out some travelers checks which would take time, so he continued with his business.

He then emptied his right front trouser pocket, then his jacket pockets. Joyce McLeod got a scoop, placed all the coins

101

in it and went to the rear of her work area to a coin sorter, dropping the coins into the top of that piece of machinery. When it had completed its job, and with the total registering on a small screen, Joyce then selected a number of currency bills with a bit of change and gave it to the young guy. He left.

I stepped to the window and said to Joyce, "Must have been a big poker game to have all that change."

She replied with a grin, "Yes, it's too bad that the legal drinking age isn't twenty one in this state anymore, did you smell the booze on him?"

"Regretfully." I said, But you know there's not a darn thing we can do about that now, with the bleeding hearts having their way last year in the legislature. He didn't appear drunk, though, it's just that he must have been at it heavily last night or early into the morning."

I completed my transaction and left the bank. "See you, Joyce."

The time of my arrival was fixed in my mind as I had left police headquarters at about 3:10 P.M. and noted the clock on the wall behind Joyce McLeod to be 3:20 P.M. when I arrived at the bank.

The next day, April 14th, as I was returning to the Narco office in the Detective Bureau, I was called into his office by Inspector Pound. I had just given testimony in a drug case in District Court and was in a bit of a testy mood after one hour on the stand, with the assistant county attorney prosecuting the case offering little in the way of objection to the irrelevant, repetitious questioning by the defense attorney.

"Were you at the Northern City National Bank yesterday?" He asked.

"Yes", I answered, thinking he was going to climb on my case for doing PB, (personal business), during work hours.

"Can you recall the approximate time?"

"Look, Inspector, I'm working 'till six every day, because of court and because we are also doing some undercover buys with the DEA, that's the only chance I would have to get travelers checks for my trip to D.C. day after tomorrow." I said emphatically.

"Whoa", he said, "That's not what I'm leading up to. We had an incident that Jim Bujold and Tom Ehle are working on and I don't want to color your thinking before I tell you what it's about, so if you can recall the time, it will help."

"3:20 P.M. exactly".

"You positive?"

Sure, there was a young guy in front of me cashing in a couple pockets full of coins with Joyce McLeod, the teller."

At that time, Detective Sergeant Tom Ehle, "Mojo" to some of his fellow cops, approached me and asked if I could identify the person cashing in the coins.

"I'm sure I can."

Tom then laid out six photos of young men similar in appearance and I identified the photo of Barry Eugene Hanson.

Pound and Ehle then told me what details were available on a homicide of a young female which had occurred that previous afternoon.

The young woman, not quite twenty, was sharing an apartment with a young man who was gainfully employed doing an apprenticeship as a butcher in a shop owned by his father and uncle, Bob and Dick Wrazidlo, two merchants well known for high quality meats as well as their sponsorship of champion softball, football and basketball teams.

While her boyfriend, the apprentice, was working, neighbors saw an acquaintance of his go into the apartment at about 1 P.M.

When the apprentice came home shortly after 5 P.M., he found his girlfriend lying on her bed, naked and dead. In shock, but being of strong character, he immediately called the police. Uniform patrol units as well as detectives responded.

When Detective Sergeant Jim Bujold canvassed the immediate neighbors in the apartment building, it didn't take him long to learn of the visit between 1 P.M. and 1:50 P.M. that afternoon.

Returning to the apartment and upon interviewing the boyfriend, he asked, "Do you know a guy who goes by the name of Barry?'

"Yes, he's sort of a friend, Barry Hanson is his name. We've known each other for a few months and have a been together once in a while. Why do you ask?"

"No real reason, just tossing some names at you for now," said Bujold, "does he ever visit you at the apartment?"

"Sure, but only when I'm here. If you don't mind, can we do this a little later? I can't think straight. We were planning to marry. Who in heaven's name would want to kill her? She was such a quiet person."

"We'd really want to try to get some answers now. It may help us get to the bottom of this quicker if you can force yourself to bear with us just a few minutes more." said Bujold.

During this time a Deputy Medical Examiner had arrived and was going about his business.

"I want to notify her parents, they live in another city and will die when they hear this." moaned the apprentice.

"We'll do that, just give us their name, address and phone number and we will have the police in that town speak to them personally rather than by phone." Said a sympathetic Bujold, himself a father several times. He continued, "Can you look around the apartment to see if anything is missing, anything at all that you know is out of place?"

The apprentice, accompanied by Bujold, commenced to go from room to room seeing nothing amiss, but avoided the girls bedroom where the Deputy Medical Examiner was just finishing his exam of the body and the crime scene.

"We can wait a few minutes until he's done and have her brought to the morgue, then you can look around in there, okay?" Asked Bujold.

"Okay."

The Deputy Medical Examiner emerged from the bedroom, called Bujold and Ehle into another room, and told them that his preliminary exam indicated strangulation, no rape, but sexual assault of another kind. "The assailant, apparently wanting to force sex on her, lost it when she refused, strangled her, then disrobed her, masturbated and obviously ejaculated semen all over her upper torso," he said, adding, "she appears to have some flesh under her fingernails, but we won't touch that until we do our work at the morgue. I've already collected a sample of the fluid from her torso."

"Thanks doctor," said Ehle, "is there anything else?"

"Yes, I notice a large clear glass jar, about a gallon size, lying on its side near the foot of the bed. I didn't touch it, but you might want to ask the boyfriend about that. I've got a mortuary crew standing by outside to take her to the morgue if you guys have enough photos of her and the room, okay?"

"Thanks doctor," both detectives said almost simultaneously.

After the victim had been taken by the morticians, Bujold and Ehle led the apprentice into the bedroom and, as he looked around, he immediately spotted the large glass jar and said, "The money!"

"What money?" asked Ehle.

"She's a waitress in a coffee shop over on Fourth Street, and she has been throwing her tip money in the jar every day which is what I do with tips from the butcher shop."

They now had a suspect and evidence, i.e., the semen, as well as the large amount of missing coins which could prove important.

The next day sergeants Bujold and Ehle, with assistance from a couple other detectives, began a systematic survey of banks starting with the Park State Bank in the Morgan Park neighborhood, on into the several banks in West Duluth, progressing though Lincoln Park and finally into the downtown business district, while their counterparts started in the east extreme section of the city, Lakeside, and worked their way west, toward downtown.

At the Northern City National Bank in mid afternoon, while checking the dozen or so tellers at their booths, Tom Ehle approached Joyce McLeod and after identifying himself, asked, "Has there been anybody at your counter cashing in or depositing a large amount of money in coins?"

"Matter of fact, yes, a young man yesterday afternoon, but why don't you talk with Eli Miletich about that, he was right behind him in the line?" She responded.

Momentarily and pleasantly surprised, Ehle recovered and asked if she could identify that person from several photo's he laid out before her.

She immediately picked Barry Eugene Hanson.

After obtaining a written witness statement from Joyce, Ehle returned to the Detective Bureau to pass on his findings to Pound, whereupon I just happened to be returning from court.

Good luck was abounding all over the place but then unnecessary caution, for whatever reason, took hold.

The Deputy Medical Examiner had established the approximate time of death as only several hours prior to the discovery of the victims body. Witnesses had placed Barry Eugene Hanson at the scene from one o'clock to one fifty that afternoon. Money in the form of coins was missing and two credible witnesses had seen Hanson exchange a large amount of coins for currency at a downtown bank within an hour and one half of his departure from where her body was later found in the apartment.

Probable cause, in sufficient volume, existed to believe that the suspect had committed the crime to justify a request for an arrest warrant, but either inexperience in handling such cases, or the desire for extended press coverage prevailed. On this one I choose to subscribe to the former.

Instead of going for an arrest warrant, Pound directed the detectives working on the case to find the suspect and establish a 'round the clock surveillance' on him. I'm not too sure what the thinking was, but it smacks of J. Conan Doyle's Sherlock Holmes, 'give the suspect enough rope and he will hang himself' writings. It didn't work!

The suspect became aware early on that he had company wherever he went, so he played some mind games. Go into a grocery store, walk out the back door. Go visit his mother, to a movie, see the previews and leave. These were daily occurrences and still no move to arrest based on solid evidence.

At one point I stopped in Pound's office and asked "Ray, you actually have enough probable cause to move on this guy now, why not do so? With what you have, you don't need a statement, but if he is booked, you might see some jailhouse psychology take hold."

"Eli, I want this guy to stub his toe and then we can really stick it to him where no defense attorney can argue that we don't have a good case."

"What more can you expect? I asked in frustration.

"I don't know, but we've got time. He's been staying at his mothers out on Indian Point, we know that. His father lives in some small town in the Ozarks in southern Missouri, and if he attempts to leave, then we'll grab him."

I didn't then, nor do I now, understand the logic of that thinking, but suffice it to say, one day Barry Eugene Hanson walked out of his mothers home, north to Grand Avenue, east on Grand and turned into the west entrance of the Duluth Zoo, a multi acre facility housing a wide variety of creatures of the wild.

The guys on the loose surveillance dutifully reported his travels to their supervisors and were advised by Pound, through those supervisors, to wait near the entrances to the Zoo to see what he does next.

Barry Eugene Hanson simply continued walking through the Zoo property, north up the steeply sloped hillside until he got to a clearing leading to southbound Interstate 35, climbed over the Zoo fence and hitchhiked a ride as far as Minneapolis. In a subsequent series of rides, he continued all the way to his fathers hillbilly home in the Ozarks.

The surveillance team, after sitting in place for several hours, could possibly be still sitting there today if someone had not told the Inspector that he had been had.

Bujold, through an informant, learned of Hanson's whereabouts in a few weeks and reported this to Pound who, after thinking it over, sent Bujold to that small Ozark town to look for Hanson and hopefully get help from the local cops.

Jim Bujold, a calm easy going guy, who is not fearful of any assignment, met open hostility from the Ozark neighbors of Barry Eugene Hanson's father as well, to a limited degree, from local law enforcement people. Bujold later described them as 'circling the wagons' for one of their own.

Concerned, in part, for his own safety, he left, but first advised the local sheriff to tell Barry Eugene Hanson, when he sees him, to turn himself in.

Hanson stayed in Missouri for over one year and suddenly appeared on the charges in Duluth.

*Eli J. Miletich*

One might ask what new evidence was discovered in the one year since the murder? Nothing!

A short trial and a crafty lawyer hammering away at police indecision and ineptness, convinced the jury that Barry Eugene Hanson must be innocent, else why did the police wait so long?

Barry Eugene Hanson was acquitted.

There are also people who lose because they throw all caution to the wind.

Chapter Nine

When I was a kid growing up in a West Duluth neighborhood known by the name of the main thoroughfare passing through it, Raleigh Street, the most feared and despised representatives of government were the police.

To a community mostly made up of European immigrants and their offspring, the representatives of law enforcement, i.e., the policia, polis, policajac, milicija, or cops, were the oppressors, and their words and actions not to be challenged in the old country.

People who lived in the neighborhood usually spoke in terms of admiration about their neighbors and surroundings, and referred to themselves as being from "The Street" with pride and, yes, a certain degree of cockiness which was easily seen by outsiders. Though family was always number one, the environment of the neighborhood had a lasting impact on my developing years.

Immigrants from the Scandinavian countries, prior to the turn of the 20th Century, were among the first to populate and

*Eli J. Miletich*

propagate "The Street", and names such as Peterson, Johnson, Anderson, Nellis, Olson, Christianson, Chilstrand, adorned the mail boxes.

As was usually the case with people new to a land, they suffered prejudices at the hands of those of long standing residency in the city. Jobs were of the menial kind; servants, digging ditches for the citys' new sewer system, working the saw mills which dotted the city shoreline on Lake Superior, sweating away their lifeblood to provide their kids a better living standard than that which they left in Europe.

Children of those immigrants, beneficiaries of a growing public education system, soon moved into the professional and skilled trades positions a developing economy produced.

The Irish followed and went through the same indignities and subsequent accomplishments. Family names such as O'Brien, McNulty, Rollins, Donahue, O'Neil, Cullins, became common for blocks.

But it was before and after World War One that "The Street" saw the largest wave of immigrants arrive from central and southern Europe.

Because a true melting pot effect was now in place in the neighborhood, a U.S. Postal Carrier, most likely a descendant of the earlier arrivals, had to learn names such as DeGrio, Briski, Vrdoljak, Ossana, Rico, Bushko, Kurtovich, Amatuzio, Colalillo, Chumich, Sackette, Conito, Bordeau, Heitala, Sisto, Fajdetich, Francisco, Boyat, Parendo, Skorich, Mikrut, Moran, Ujdur, Vitich, Foubister, Petrich, Rish, Colich, Glibota, Vegar, DeBasio, Puglisi, Bullyan, Mendesh, Mlikota, Glamuzina, Opacak, Sisto, Modrich, Sabich, Carich, Mucilli, Zivkovich, Udovich, and countless others in addition to the Swedes, Norwegians and Irish.

The male members of those families found jobs in the new U.S Steel and Interlake Iron steel mills being constructed. Blast furnace and coke ovens work was the destiny for most.

During my early years, our regular mail carrier was a man named George Dunleavy, a son of Irish immigrants, and he not only could rattle off those funny sounding names to perfection, he was able to converse, in a limited fashion, with some some of the residents in their native tongues. I also remember many a cold, blustery winter day when, our home being half way through his route, my father, out sawing firewood, would invite Mr. Dunleavy to stop for a quick warm up of rakija.

"The Street" settled by people of various backgrounds who learned to understand, tolerate and oftentimes defend each others ethnic, cultural and racial traditions, became synonymous with what this country is all about. It meant people who could tough out the most adverse conditions and situations; it meant togetherness; it meant lovely respected women; it meant rough and tough youngsters from whose midst came the most spirited and competitive athletic teams in the city including several of the greatest athletes in its history, such as a middleweight title contender, Angelo Puglisi. All around athletes just didn't come any better than brothers Zivko "Zeke" and Milt "Meecho" Boyat.

From that proud neighborhood came future educators, skilled tradesmen, physicians, scientists, firefighters, cops, attorneys, a federal judge, business leaders, including the founder of one of the country's largest synthetic oil producers and scores of folks who worked with their minds, backs and hands.

One individual of whom the neighbors share a great pride is Mike Colalillo, whose parents came from Italy. As a nineteen year old soldier he distinguished himself by extraordinary deeds of valor and heroism in Germany during World War II, for which he was awarded the nations highest military honor, the Congressional Medal of Honor, presented to him by President Harry S. Truman in 1945.

I mention the aforesaid, including the names, and ask your indulgence for that, because it illustrates the diversity and strength of the people who lived in the neighborhood; besides, this is my story!

----

A coincidence in history and politics occurred around the same time period as the latest arrivals to the shores of this country in the early part of the twentieth century. Prohibition.

Because consumption of alcoholic beverages was traditionally a part of their lives, particularly having wine with meals many, if not most, immigrants from southern Europe, in Duluth, as in the rest of the land, felt prohibition was a direct affront to them.

In many homes wine was produced in one hundred gallon barrels and, in some instances, wine produced in excess of family needs for the ensuing year was sold to neighbors who did not crush grapes. A byproduct of the wine making process was the distillation of mash from the grapes to make rakija, the very unique Slavic brandy.

As is common with other illegal activities, enterprising minds saw that if they concentrated on production and sale, there were dollars aplenty to be made.

Primary responsibility for enforcement of this unpopular law fell on the local police departments, thus the attitude among the immigrants about the police as the instrument of oppression was enhanced.

If the police were to be negatively involved with their personal, innocent sipping of a glass, then how could one not be fearful of police involvement in their everyday lives. Prohibition ended in 1933, several years before my birth, but stories abound about its' aftermath and the continued police harassment.

I recall, as a ten or eleven year old, shortly after the second world war, setting up our portable shoe shine stand with Ron Rico and Tony Briski, on the corner of 56th and Raleigh, near the North Pole Bar, and clowning around with kids my size or age who also just hung around on Saturday afternoons. We would take turns watching "chiggers" if the cops were seen driving our way, while the older guys played craps, dice, on a concrete slab alongside the Tappa Keg Inn, next door to the North Pole. The guys in the nickel, dime dice game were war veterans, having put their lives on the line for their country and, in their minds, a bit of social gambling was recreational, after all, they had been permitted to do it during their months of service in foreign lands.

On the other hand, being one of the kids growing up on "The Street" who knew every kid and their family, and where they lived, for blocks around, I saw some of the wrongs the police of that era committed.

The Purity Squad, as it was called until a name change in the early fifties, now, Vice Squad, was responsible for investigation of illegal sales of alcohol, gambling, prostitution and other related vices. Officers assigned to that detail always worked in plain clothes but they were known to all in as much as their black cars with the long whip antennas set them apart from the others.

As kids, it was common for us to get up a game of 'kick the stick', 'kick the can', 'inny-inny-aye over' or even '500 softball' in any vacant lot or, in most cases, an alley. One of the nicest alleys, because it was unpaved and wider than others, was directly behind the Sisto's home which was across the alley from one of the city's most productive and prosperous bootleggers, an otherwise honest, god fearing man.

Seeking out prohibited Sunday sales of alcoholic beverages, and the unlicensed serving of alcohol were the primary chores of the Purity Squad in those days. The high price of booze on the retail market provided the incentive for bootleggers to continue with their lucrative business, naturally at discount prices.

On a number of occasions the plain black cars with the whip antenna would come slowly down the alley where we were playing. Seeing us, they would shout something like, "You damn kids, we keep getting calls from neighbors about you playing in this alley. Go down to the playground!" If by chance some unlucky kid had his back to them as their car crept down the alley he could, and in many instances did, get a swift kick in the butt for emphasis.

Disappearing quickly, but not far, we would conduct our own surveillance and watch the Purity Squad guys emerge from their car, walk to the rear of the bootleggers house, knock, and be admitted and seated in the fully enclosed glass sun porch. The bootlegger, or a member of his family, would then proceed to serve them just as if they were in a licensed tavern or bar. Believe it, they were not acting in an undercover role, developing a case for prosecution, because we witnessed this many times. A couple of the most notorious, in our minds, were guys named Brandenhoff and Mayville. It was the times.

We did have revenge of sorts once in a while.

If the situation was right, when the Purity Squad guys were comfortably seated and served, one or two of the more daring kids would sneak back, running from backside of one garage to another until next to their vehicle. We'd then let air out of all four tires.

When they emerged from having their libation in a half hour or more, we were amused by their frustration and anger. Naturally they had some choice words for their unseen culprits, unseen because it usually was about dusk for their visits to the bootlegger. The next step for them was to call Ceyborske's Sinclair Service Station to come pump up the tires.

Years later, when I was a young cop myself and attended a retirement party at the old Fitger's Brewery Tap Room for some officers who were leaving the department, I met one of those Purity Squad guys, Mayville. He had retired several years earlier. The newer guys wore name tags so others would catch our names.

He walked up to me and said, "Aren't you one of those smart-ass kids from Raleigh Street that we used to kick in the ass once in a while?"

"Yeah, and aren't you one one of the guys who's tires we used to flatten in the alley behind the bootleggers when you went in to drink illegal, free booze?"

124

"No, we were just working on a case against the guy," he replied.

"Once every other week?"

"Well, that was the way things were in those days," he laughed.

Many other times, being alley rats that we were, we also observed marked patrol cars pull up in the parking lot at the rear of the North Pole Bar, with both officers walking in, ushered into the back room, an office, and served drinks. Our observation point for these activities was a couple of old rain barrels stacked up under that office window about seven feet above the ground.

However, it wasn't only the police who practiced this hypocrisy

Quite often we watched as a big Cadillac drove right up to the rear of the bootleggers garage and Municipal Court Judge Royal Bouschor went in to imbibe with his good friend serving him. The irony of this all is that about once every two years that bootlegger would be arrested, charged and fined about $100 in Municipal Court and be back in business the next day.

That bootlegger used to state in his learned English with a strong Slavic accent, "I ben in dees kontry tirty years and neber hab bleesters na mine hands. I do my beesnis and vonce in vile pay mine texes in court."

The man, despite his illegal activities, was arguably more honest than the cops and judge who drank his product.

Such was life growing up on "The Street."

Don't trust lawyers, politicians or cops!

The guys working the Congdon murder case, with the exception of Pound and Yagoda, were mostly devoid of humor and much too intense in going after information and evidence.

Police work is not without its humorous instances. In fact, if you don't find humor in some of the cases and investigations you're working on, you may get too wound up in the job and, that's stressful and can be harmful to the health. Many professions utilize humor to relieve stress, an example might be professionals such as surgeons who are notorious for operating room humor.

In the group with whom I learned and developed into police work, who started in the late 50's and early 60's, there was a type of humor and humility that seems to be rare on the job now.

When you're working as close as cops are accustomed to, you learn each others life history and idiosyncrasies.

For example, I was a Medic in the Army and quite naturally would talk about my army career occasionally during BS sessions with various partners. It would get to the point that sometimes a tale told to a partner would be unwittingly repeated to him a few months later. "Yeah, I know, you were an Army Medic." Would be the comment. Or perhaps at the scene of a serious vehicular accident or a homicide, I would be asked to determine the cause of death with, "You were an old Army Medic, weren't you?"

One day in May, in fact it was Memorial Day, shortly after I had been promoted to Lieutenant and temporarily assigned to the Detective Bureau as a supervisor, a call came in from a district patrol squad in West Duluth for a detective to respond to a private residence where an elderly woman had been found dead by her son in law who in turn called the police.

After giving the assignment to Sergeant Dan Price, I remembered that he was working alone, as his partner was on vacation, and since other detectives were tied up on cases, I asked Dan if he could use some company, which, of course, he did.

Before leaving headquarters I advised the Desk Officer of my whereabouts and that I could be reached by walkie-talkie if needed. We figured that after we checked out this DOA and told the squad, "Yup, she's dead." we'd stop for a cup of coffee and a sandwich.

It didn't work out quite that way.

Upon our arrival at the home on North 63rd Avenue West, we were brought into the dining room where we noted the deceased, lying face down on the floor, her whole upper torso and head encircled by a pool of dark red blood.

Papers found on a desk in that room told us her name was Ella Johnson. She was 83 years old and had been under a doctor's care for high blood pressure. Her medications were also on that desk. She was a widow and had a daughter who lived with the son in law about eight blocks from her.

The patrol officers advised us that a Deputy Medical Examiner had been notified and was responding.

They also told us that the son in law was there when they arrived, but that he had gone home to comfort his wife.

Mrs. Johnson was a very neat housekeeper. The place was immaculate. Everything was clean and the furniture dusted and polished. To use the old cliche, you could literally eat a meal off the kitchen floor. All was orderly.

Her position, in the middle of the dining room floor, was as if she had possibly suffered a stroke and fell face first on the floor, perhaps breaking her nose or suffering other serious cuts about the face, hence all the blood.

Or maybe she suffered a hemorrhage passed out and fell flat on her face.

Ella Johnson was wearing the kind of house dress that elderly women find fashionable, and a button down knit sweater with a high collar. Her cane, one of those claw at the bottom aluminum walking sticks, was lying alongside her body.

In any event, her death appeared to be from natural causes, absent any sign of struggle or violence.

Waiting for the Deputy Medical Examiner to show got a bit boring, and after we finished discussing the Twins loss to the Yankees the day before, we resorted to guessing as to the cause of death.

The two uniform officers were in agreement that she had a stroke, fell, broke her nose, bled, and died there because of her age and frail condition before her son in law found her.

Dan Price suggested hemorrhage but said, "What do you say, you're the one who always talks about being an old Army medic. You're the self proclaimed expert!"

"Well, " I said studiously, "I have to go along with the hemorrhage theory, only I'd say it was what is described as a massive cerebral hemorrhage, especially with all that blood around the whole upper part of her body."

"Expert, huh," snorted Price.

Minutes later Dr. Bob Kleismet arrived and, after we briefed him, I asked him to give us his preliminary thoughts as to cause of death, pointing out my "old Army Medic" opinion. Surprisingly, he said he tended to agree.

"But, fellows," he said, "why don't we turn her over on her back so we can see if she broke any facial bones when she fell, and maybe we can then get a better picture of what happened. Of course, we need to do an autopsy, as you well know."

With that we all knelt by the body so that we could uniformly turn her over.

One of the uniform guys took her legs; Price her hips; Dr. Kleismet her torso and I, her head.

"Now, on the count of three," said the doctor.

When he reached three, we slowly and gently started to turn the body over and, as we did, her head started to tilt back into my hands, revealing a gaping hole where her Adams Apple, her throat, should have been. Only the flesh at the back of the neck was keeping the head from being totally separated from the torso. Someone had apparently come up from behind her, put a knee to her back, forced her to the floor and slit her throat. The high collar on her knit sweater had concealed the wound from us until we turned her over.

The Deputy Medical Examiner looked at me in all seriousness and said, "Looks like you and I are going to lose our license to practice medicine!"

"Not me, Doc, I'm just an old Army Medic enlisted man, you're the MD," I quickly retorted.

A closer look by Dr. Kleismet revealed that a very sharp instrument had been used, such as a fish knife or even a scalpel, although, he surmised, because of her age and delicate condition, it didn't necessarily take a person of great strength to commit the murder.

Identification Tech's were called to the home to perform the necessary crime scene work now that we knew we had a homicide. We also undertook a search for the weapon, in the event it was in the home. Perhaps it was one of her own kitchen cutlery. Nothing was found.

We had metal detectors brought out so that a search of the yard could be conducted, and a K-Nine unit also checked out a wooded area to the rear of the property. Nothing!

We interviewed the daughter. She told us that she had been ill and hadn't been able to see her mother in weeks but that her husband was checking on her every morning at about ten o'clock.

On this day he made a booze run, going to a liquor store for a case of beer and a couple bottles of brandy before going to her mothers, where he said he found her on the floor.

Upon interviewing the son in law, we got basically the same story, except he did acknowledge that he had incurred her wrath from time to time because of his trips to the liquor store. She felt that this was doing her daughter no good and, in fact, making her an alcoholic.

Questioning him in greater detail, we learned that she wasn't terribly pleasant when berating his perceived drinking problem. Rather, it seemed that she was a thorn in his side.

Knowing the danger to an investigation if tunnel vision is utilized when looking for suspects, we did feel that we should either rule him in or out as a suspect. Thus, we offered him a polygraph test. An appointment was made for the following day. He was asked not to have any of his favorite beverages prior to coming down to the PD.

He took the test and failed. However, he made no admissions and was sent home to his wife, hopefully to stew about it for a while.

The next day we received a call from his physician who was treating him for terminal cancer. Our suspect was under daily medication for his ailment, and we were advised by the doctor that the medication could have influenced the polygraph results. The County Attorneys office, when contacted by the doctor, agreed. Since polygraph results are not admissible this was a moot point. The investigation languished.

In August, one of the other detectives received a call from some neighbor kids who were taking a shortcut through Ella Johnsons' back yard when they found a fish cleaning knife stuck into the ground at the base of a large oak tree. They said it was a very sharp and had just a bit of rust on it. It was found in plain sight, not concealed in any way. The detective retrieved it and when he called to make an appointment to talk with the son in law, he learned that he had passed away, from Cancer, about four days prior to the knife being found. Lab tests showed traces of human blood on the knife. No other evidence or suspects were ever developed.

---

Fred Sowl is a big, strong, raw boned guy with super intelligence. What takes others three to four minutes to perceive and understand, he will latch on to in seconds. He also has a great sense of right and wrong. Fred started on the job about a year after me, and we worked on the same patrol group for a number of years, as well as within the Detective Bureau.

Fred had also been on the Police Union Executive Board during the time I was Union president, so we had quite an extensive working relationship.

He, Sowl, had been an Ironworker prior to coming on the Police Department and, loved to tell Ironworker stories.

Ironworkers are those daring guys who walk around on steel beams of buildings under construction. Many of those buildings are multi floors.

There was another Ironworker that several of us knew who lived in West Duluth, where many of us on the department came from, and whom we used as a fall guy when we wanted to rib Fred about his Ironworker career. The guy's name was Billy Hendrickson. He had a reputation as being among the best of the best.

So it came to pass that when Fred Sowl would mention something about his previous career, one of us, usually Steve Kurtovich, Dan Price, Gene Sisto or me, would say something like, "You know, I was talking with Billy Hendrickson last week and he says that you were a horse shit Ironworker, that you were too reckless. He says that the rest of the Ironworkers were afraid you might slip and take a dive from a thirty or forty story job, so they gave you a job on the ground, stoking a fire, heating rivets. He also says that your nickname is "Rivets."

Initially Fred did not know that we were stroking him, and his pride would be slightly wounded. He would respond by saying, "I wonder why Billy would say that about me, he knows that I worked some of the big jobs and had no problem. I can't figure that out."

We would repeat that line a few times to others until we thought it was getting old, so we let Fred know that his old work partner had never made such claims, nor had any of us talked with Billy recently.

Fred then confessed that he had felt so bad that Billy would be saying those things that the next time he saw him he was going to tell him to knock it off.

Well, one year on Good Friday, we had a search warrant for an upstairs apartment of a duplex at 24 East 2nd Street, on the hillside just above the downtown business district, across from old Central High School.

An informant had made several controlled buys of small amounts of heroin from a suspect. We had wanted the informant to make an introduction of an undercover agent to the dealer so that we could make what is called a buy-bust.

The informant said that the dealer, a Hippie named Schneider, did not want any new faces coming around, so we decided that we could not wait any longer and applied for a search warrant.

We put together a search team of guys from our Narco-Vice Unit and several others from the Detective Bureau. Fred Sowl was one of the guys from that division.

When we got to that upstairs apartment in the middle of the afternoon, we quietly tried the door handle. It would not turn. We did have a warrant which authorized a "no knock search", so I reared back and kicked. No one was home. We found out later that the informant had developed a guilty conscience and had tipped off the dealer that cops were about to raid his place and he had cleared out only minutes before we got there. He was arrested some months later in Boston for selling cocaine to an undercover agent.

Anyway, after entering, we proceeded to search the entire apartment, with officers fanning out into the several rooms.

There was a cubbyhole door in the kitchen ceiling going into the attic, so I found a couple chairs, stacked them up to raise me to a level where I could hoist myself up into the attic.

Once in the attic, there was a low sloped roof line, with the rafters going about six feet at the tallest down to a few inches, one had to walk along the ceiling joists in a crouch if you wanted to check out the far reaches of the attic.

I crouched and walked along the joists as far as I could, until there was no more room to walk.

Using my flashlight, and almost in a crawl, I noted that nothing in the dust appeared to be new or disturbed. I shouted down to the kitchen, "Who wants to trade with me?"

Fred Sowl said he would.

When conducting a search, it's a good idea to swap places with another officer who has completed his search, because

*Eli J. Miletich*

we're all human and what one set of eyes misses, another may see. It's surprising how effective that is.

When Fred started in the attic, I went into the kitchen.

I began by looking into the narrow area behind the paneling at the rear of the stove, then moved into the pantry. All of a sudden we heard a loud crash coming from the direction of the living room where Gene Sisto and Denny Lepak were searching. Had someone been hiding in a closet and was now making a run for it?

Running out of the kitchen, through the dining room and into the adjoining living room, I looked up at the ceiling and saw a large hole, about five feet in diameter, with laths and plaster hanging around the edges, and in the middle of the hole, the two huge, long legs of Fred Sowl. There was a mess of plaster on the floor beneath him.

Gene Sisto was standing off to the side, a bemused look on his face, and said, "And you claim to have been an Ironworker," to roars of laughter from all taking part in the search.

For a guy who normally doesn't cuss, Fred did.

Sowl had walked those narrow ceiling joists, only two inches wide, and sixteen inches apart, about five feet deeper into the attic than I had, despite being bigger physically than I, and when he turned to go back to the cubbyhole, one of his feet slipped off the joist and, crash. He ended up straddling the joist like a bronc rider. Fortunately for him there were no nails sticking up. You can bet he still hasn't heard the last of that tale. At least our version of it.

A postscript to this incident is that someone who had seen us going into the apartment building and knew the landlady, a very obese slumlord who owned a number of apartment buildings bordering the downtown, called to tell her that the police were at one of her buildings.

Curiosity forced her to come over to see what we were up to.

When she came waddling up the stairs, huffing and puffing from the climb, she identified herself to the officer at the door to the apartment, Joe Sinnott, and he allowed her to enter. As she stepped into the the apartment, she looked into the living room, saw the plaster on the floor and the large hole in the ceiling and

*Eli J. Miletich*

said, "Look at what those damn hippies have done to my ceiling!"

I quickly explained what had happened and advised her to contact the City Attorney's office to file a claim for damages. She wasted no time doing so as we later learned from the City Claims Investigator assigned to the matter.

---

Every cop knows that insults, cursing, and even an occasional punch in the nose, kick in groin or, even worse but rarely, getting killed, goes with the job. There are times when it is downright humorous, and others when tragic.

When I was about three years on the job and partnered with a guy who was an old high school football opponent, Nick Popovich, we often tried to find a humorous side to the many calls we were dispatched to or even those we developed on our own initiative.

Nick was an outstanding high school athlete at Morgan Park, especially in football. He stood about six feet one inches and was built like the proverbial farm, brick out house; no one got through him at his tackle position on defense, and on offense he was most often used to plow the way for running back Chuck Jasper.

Now his football team, a high school on the far western end of the city, was annually a strong competitor, but one year in particular, Nick's senior year and my junior year at Denfeld, they were rated 1st or 2nd in the state for most of the season, running over other schools in the city, and those on their schedule from outside the conference. Until they played us.

We had a so-so team of guys with a lot of heart, but not that much in skill or experience to be able to stay on the same field with Morgan Park, an undefeated powerhouse.

I also should point out that Morgan Park High School had a small school enrollment, about three hundred fifty, tenth to twelfth grades, compared to eleven hundred or so, each, in the three other city public high schools. Accordingly, the team would be lucky if they could put more than thirty in uniform in any one year as against the others who could boast forty five to fifty. In high school football, reserves can make the difference.

It was an evenly fought game, much of the action between the thirty yard lines, except for a few long bursts by Chuck

143

Jasper, one of the most talented backs in the state, and one of the best in the history of Duluth football. Morgan Park had scored both its' touchdowns on such runs by Jasper, missing the extra point try on one, and we had scored a touchdown but missed the extra point, so at the end of three quarters, it stood 13-6, Morgan Park.

After a few attempts by both teams to get something going in the fourth quarter, defense was the name of the game, and when our team had held up a furious drive, taking over on downs on our own thirty yard line, Coach Walt Hunting figured it was time to send in a play always held in reserve, called the Cathedral special in that it had worked as a surprise play some years before against Duluth's only parochial high school thus, was practiced often, but seldom used. It was run off the old single wing formation, this in the days when most high schools, colleges and especially the pros, were running the newer, flashier, T formation.

The Cathedral special was sent in from the sidelines. Lined up with the fullback about seven feet directly behind the center, the quarterback behind the right offensive guard, the right halfback behind the right tackle about four feet and the left halfback to the left of the fullback but a step in front of him, the ball gets snapped directly back to the fullback who spins and while doing so, fakes a hand off to the left halfback who runs to the right, carrying out the fake as if he has the ball. The fullback instantly runs with the ball as if to run over the right tackle position. This is when the quarterback spins around in his position and runs past the fullback who gives the ball to the quarterback who then runs deeper into his own back field, away from any defenders attempting to make a tackle. About eight to ten yards into his own backfield he turns around and looks for the left end who should be running downfield, in the clear, as the rest of the maneuvers are designed to draw most of the defense around to the right side and or toward the middle of the line. If the left end is clear, the ball is lofted to him, voila, a touchdown.

That line rush of the Park team was so powerful, that I barely had time to get set and as I spotted big Jim Jago heading past the safety and threw, I was creamed by four rushing linemen, led by none other than Nick Popovich. I was knocked back on my can, with all four taunting me as we went down. The crowd at Public Schools Stadium roared. The five of us on the ground thought it was because the play was broken up or maybe an interception.

As we got to our feet we could see downfield and Jim Jago was speeding over the goal line with the ball tucked tightly in his armpit. It was my turn then to taunt.

We kicked the extra point, and that was the way the game ended, 13-13.

This tie on their record was the only thing to keep them from being rated number one in the state, and even though it was only a high school football game long ago, it is something that is never forgotten. That's how it went with my partner, Nick Popovich, especially when he would sound off in front of the other guys about that strong "undefeated" team of the fall of 1951. Likewise, because we had competed in sports from our early youth, other members of that "undefeated" team are not permitted to forget. Even though everyone chooses different paths and careers, friendships have been maintained with many of those guys over the years, so it's easy to reminisce about the old times when meeting up with guys like LeRoy Larson, Wally Puchalla, Jerry Nelson, Bob Kervina, Billy Papike, Joe Jukich, and Jim Hickey, all multiple sport athletes.

Now, it was just about the time that we were having a strong discussion about that game when we got the call, "Squad 46".

Our response. "Go ahead".

"Squad 46, go to 1108 West 2nd Street, reference a domestic assault."

"10-04, we're on our way."

We were clear from our last call on the east end of our assigned district, so we moved out. The call had come across at 1:35 A.M., the bewitching hour as we liked to call it, because that was when the guy came home from a night of bar hopping and after all that drinking it magically made him smarter, tougher and above all, more masterful of his spouse; or, not to forget, better able to cope with any cops who might come into his pathway.

We got to the curb in front of the residence in less than four minutes. It was a warm summer night, and when we stepped out of our squad car, we could hear the woman screaming, "There's the cops now, you bastard!"

The home had a glassed in sun porch, with a screen door and the interior, main entry, door was wide open. "Screw you and the cops!" he shouted. "I didn't lay a hand on you, you're the one who broke my nose!"

As we got to the screen door, I rang the door bell, and a female voice hollered, "Come on in." The male voice, from another direction to the left, inside the house shouted, "Don't come in this fucking house without a warrant."

One of the last things a cop does is to go into a situation such as a domestic where no one from inside the home opens the door for you and you don't see the person who invites you in. It's hazardous and potentially dangerous. She called out again, "Come on in, I'm in the kitchen, and he's in the living room, but he's hurt."

We took the chance that someone was not hiding behind the main entry door, and very quietly opened the screen door and on our tip toes, walked through the porch until we could see through the open door to a dining room and into the kitchen where the woman, in her house coat, was leaning back against the stove. Off to our left in the living room, sitting on the couch, was the male who was holding a large towel to his face. By now the towel, which was white, was saturated with blood apparently from the man's nose.

I went into the kitchen and spoke with the woman while Nick tended to the man.

"What happened?" I asked. "What is your name and what is his?"

"His name is Angelo and mine is Teresa. The son of a bitch was out drinking with his buddies, maybe even whoring, and he comes home about a half hour ago, drunk and wanting to know where his supper is. I told him to go back where he was all night and get his supper. He started pushing, slapping and punching me. I ran into the kitchen and he followed me. Just look at my face."

I had already noted the black and blue welts on both cheeks and the right eye almost shut.

"He kept punching and had me bent backward over the stove. I was trying to keep my balance with my arms and

149

suddenly I touched the frying pan." She pointed to a large, heavy, cast iron skillet. "I grabbed the handle and swung it around at his face and smashed his nose. Get the son of a bitch out of here and take him to jail."

"Ma'am, under the ordinance, this amounts to a misdemeanor offense, and we can't arrest for such an offense which we did not witness, but we can take him to a hospital to get his nose looked at and tended to, then maybe he can take a cheap hotel or motel room to sleep it off for the night. You two can talk it over later in the morning. Things will look different then."

That was the way that domestics were handled in most cities in the country for decades.

"I just want him out of here, do your job. Don't be assholes like him."

I walked into the living room where Nick was trying to get Angelo to stand up. Nick was telling him that we were going to take him to St. Mary's Hospital Emergency Room, the closest from that location, to get him some medical attention. As long as he could walk we felt that we could extend ourselves and not call an ambulance, saving the poor geek a few bucks.

I asked him to show me the damage to his nose. He cooperated by taking the towel down briefly, but the blood continued to come out in long spurts. I have played organized football and hockey a good many years of my life, saw numerous injuries, especially facial, but have never seen a nose displaced such as that of Angelo's. The cartilage was positioned under his left eye and the only thing protruding from the center of his face was the bridge of the nose. And, man, was he bleeding. "C'mon, we'll give you a ride to the hospital emergency room." I said.

Nick attempted to take hold of him by one arm and I, the other. At that time Angelo straightened out and started swinging his arms wildly, dropping the towel, blood spurting all over the living room and both officers.

Now we were in a situation where the guy we wanted to assist was battling us, so we had to try to subdue him. It was at that instant Teresa came running out of the kitchen, cursing at us, "Don't hurt him, you bastards", hitting me on top of the head with that cast iron skillet. I was dazed and saw stars, but hung on to Angelo.

Good supervision is a hallmark or the Duluth Police Department and it showed in that next second. One of our shift sergeants who had noted the domestic call we had been dispatched to, and the fact that we had not cleared from the scene as yet, decided to check on our status. He appeared at the door just as Teresa had struck me on the head.

LeRoy Martin, the sergeant, immediately ran and disarmed Teresa, shaking the skillet from her hand. He placed her in cuffs and we did the same with Angelo.

Another patrol unit was called for assistance and they brought Teresa to the county jail where she was booked for assault on a police officer.

We drove Angelo to St. Mary's, Hospital Emergency Room where his nose was reset by doctors, the bleeding cauterized and packed with gauze. We waited patiently for two hours and, when they were done with him, he also went to county jail.

We both had to take a half hour off to wash up and change uniforms.

Among the many domestic or family dispatches I had responded to in my career, that one always stood out as an example of how the officers need authority to assertively act, and how a victim can turn on the officers in the blink of an eye. Thus, when in a position to do something about it, as Police Chief, I made a dramatic change in policy which mandates that officers make an arrest for Domestic Abuse when they see visible signs of injury to the victim or if they believe that the victim is in danger of bodily harm or death. It is the only misdemeanor for which police can make arrests despite not witnessing the offense.

It, the Domestic Abuse Arrest Policy, adapted on July 5, 1982, has served as a model for the entire U.S. and has been presented the prestigious John F. Kennedy School of Government/Ford Foundation award for 'Innovations In State and Local Government.'

But back to this story. For weeks after, even though the seriousness of the situation could have resulted in injuries to either of us, Nick and I laughed about how the jerk battled us when were doing him a good turn, and how his wife came to his

*Eli J. Miletich*

defense despite the fact that he had just kicked the hell out of

her and she had broken his nose.

There are times you just can't win even though you have the

best team!

## October 2.

Sergeant Pat Alexander was driving to the site off Arrowhead Road early in the A.M., when the police radio barked his squad number. Upon answering, he was told that there was a long distance caller waiting for him from Boulder, Colorado PD. "Tell him I'll call back in about twenty minutes," thinking that would be about the time it would take to turn around and get back to headquarters. He could have called from a phone booth, but he wouldn't have the resources at hand that are available at the office. It must be good though. It was only 6:15 A.M. in Colorado, and he surmised that they wouldn't be calling this early if the news was negative.

It was Shotley, the Sergeant from the day before and his voice was in a definite, upbeat tone.

"Got some good news for you, Pat," he excitedly proclaimed. Alexander noted that Shotley was now practicing a familiarity with the use of his first name. Buddies! Wouldn't have been so yesterday.

"What is it?"

"We have a missing persons report on a female from this city who fits the description of your victim to a capital T." answered Shotley.

"She was last seen about 11:30 P.M., September 28th when she left her boyfriends apartment to head to her own place," he added. "The boyfriend says she was in good spirits and had only one cocktail, a whiskey soda during the evening. He also says that when he couldn't reach her the next day at work or at her apartment, he reported her missing. We think he's clean, especially since he's been working every day and has never been to the Duluth area, not even Minnesota." Alexander smiled at Shotley's correct pronunciation of the city.

"What's her name?"

"Roxanna Livingston-Voorsanger. We don't know too much about her other than what the boyfriend tells us. Seems she was born in Iran and adopted and raised by an American family. Her father owns an architectural firm in New York City, but I think the family lives in nearby Connecticut." He then paused in his briefing to give Alexander the Voorsanger phone number in New York.

"Her adoptive family is said to be pretty secure in employment and finances and had tried a number of times to get her to return to the East Coast where they live, but she enjoyed her independence and the carefree lifestyle that went with it. She loved them, but wanted to live on her own.

She was married and divorced, had a five year old son, and was studying to be a hair stylist. The boyfriend speculated that she must have stopped at the Tropicana Lounge for cigarettes when she came across whoever killed her." Shotley concluded, then adding, "I sure feel bad about the rough way I handled the call from you yesterday."

"No sweat, just goes to show that you're human. You should see how our boss, the Chief, gets with us when he thinks we have been goofing off sometimes, and we are all friends. This info more than makes up for any misunderstanding of yesterday." said a forgiving and grateful Alexander. "We'll see if anyone in our area has or had any knowledge of her."

*Eli J. Miletich*

"Oh shit, I almost forgot in the excitement of giving you the other news!" exclaimed Shotley.

"What's that?"

"Her car is missing, too. A dark blue 1985 Toyota Station Wagon, with Colorado plates. Pat, I hope we can catch that bastard who killed her. It must have been a sadistic SOB by the way you describe it. And, it almost sounds like she must have been killed here if your Medical Examiner's estimated time of death, two days before the day on which she was found, is correct. That's about it from here, but if there is anything else that I can think of or come up with, I'll give you a quick call," finished Shotley.

"You've been a big help, thanks much, good bye." said Pat, thinking as he hung up the phone that the guy sounded sad about the murder, but relieved that there were no hard feelings over the business of the day earlier.

Alexander picked up the phone again, intending to call Medical Examiner Atteli for an update, but had second thoughts in that the victims parents needed to be notified and that was a priority to be handled now.

158

He dialed the number of Bartholomew Voorsanger's office on West 58th Street in Manhattan. A secretary answered and politely said that her boss was in a meeting with clients and was not to be disturbed unless it was someone with information about his missing daughter. He had been called by her boyfriend the day before about her missing status.

Pat advised her who he was and also that it did have to do with Roxanna. Mr. Voorsanger was connected in less than five seconds, and after being apprised of the murder, there was a minute of virtual silence, with only sobs being heard over the phone.

When the conversation resumed, Pat briefly told him of the investigation as it stood up to that time. He sobbed softly and said that he would make arrangements to fly to Duluth on the first flight out of New York the next morning, adding that he would also contact his son, Matthew, a medical student in Oregon, and have him come to assist in identifying Roxanna.

Alexander suggested, and Mr. Voorsanger agreed, that he call and leave word of his flight and arrival time in order that he,

Alexander, or someone from the Department, could pick them up.

Sergeant Alexander then went into Detective Bureau Inspector Sowl's office and briefed him.

"Pat, I think we ought to have a briefing of all officers who are involved in this investigation and do some brainstorming, do you agree?

"Can you line up a meeting for that purpose Inspector. It might appear a bit less presumptuous if the call for the meeting came from you instead of me."

"No problem, let's say 10:30 this morning, and I'll ask the Chief and Assistant Chief to sit in, it'll save me from having to brief them later."

When the briefing was completed, it was Sergeant Dick Yagoda who suggested, "How about getting a helicopter to help in the search for her car. You know, if the car is on the street, or in a lot somewhere, and not under a roof, it could be seen a lot sooner from the air, the tree cover being negligible, with the early falling of leaves this year. It could save a lot of time.

There's a lot of streets in this city. It may not bear fruit, but in addition to all our squads searching, I think it's worth a try."

Lieutenant John Hall agreed, "I think that's a good idea, but if her car has been here and is now gone, we should also get this information out to the media and press, maybe, just maybe, someone has seen the vehicle."

Great," said Alexander, "We'll do both. Dick, will you contact the State Patrol and ask them for the use of one, or even two, helicopters, if they can spare them, and if they agree, set up a search pattern for them to use. And, Lieutenant Hall, will you go to the local Toyota dealers, get a photo of a dark blue 1985 wagon, they must have one in their files; then call the press and media to a conference, give them copies of the photo and the info we have, but not the name of the victim as the family hasn't ID'd her yet. Thank those folks for their help, and stress with them that the vehicle may have been in the area, not just Duluth."

Alexander then turned to Inspector Sowl, "We'll need to have every squad on the street give this, the search for the

*Eli J. Miletich*

Toyota, the highest priority, short of responding to another homicide, rape or robbery in progress."

"Gotcha," said Sowl, then added, "Pat, we need to keep this in mind, if the person who killed her still has the car, we're taking a chance on releasing anything about it to the press. If the killer learns that we are looking for it, he will simply ditch it. I know that we need help on this, and the route we're taking is the best I can see, but we need to be aware of the potential pitfalls.

"Thanks Fred, to tell you the truth, I hadn't even thought of that, but I agree, we don't have much of a choice, especially since it looks like we don't even have the faintest idea whether or not that vehicle is even around the area now."

As it turned out, it was another good piece of police work, coupled with an accumulating series of good fortune.

Chapter Twelve

Talk of good fortune.

"You guys couldn't track an elephant in the snow," was the favorite saying of Harvey Solon to Gene Sisto and me.

Harvey, one of the last of a dying breed, an honest soul, a guy who didn't hesitate to say what was on his mind whether it was to friend or foe, and he had thousands of friends.

If he was your friend, he'd move heaven or hell to give you a hand if you had need.

He, Harvey, was my older brother Steve's age, graduating from Central High while Steve was a Denfeld man, competing in high school sports and, common in athletics on the field or court, you develop some lasting friendships. That was the situation with Harv and Steve. I'd heard of Harvey many times as I was growing up, because he was a legend of sorts, being one of a few who actually played football at four separate universities, as well as serving in the Marines during World War II and the Korean War.

It seems that in the years after the Second World War Harvey had attended school and made the team at Notre Dame, North Dakota, Minnesota, and Minnesota Duluth, though not in that particular order. Scholarships were rare in those days, but floating around from school to school on the G. I. Bill was not unusual for veterans, and Harvey was no exception, only he also played football at each in a four year span.

As a young cop, coming from a strong union family, thus active in our police union, I helped lead the fight to set up informational bannering around City Hall and, of course, the Police and Fire Departments as well as all other city facilities. Our intent was to display signs which showed our plight on wages and benefits, urging citizen and voter support for our cause.

It was the fall of 1960, and a presidential campaign was underway. At a mass meeting of all city employees early in October, I had made a motion to initiate this picketing at the arrival of Democratic candidate John F. Kennedy at the Duluth International Airport and the University of Minnesota, Duluth, where he was scheduled to speak.

The mayor, Cliff Mork, was a Democrat. Our great governor, Orville Freeman and Senator Hubert H. Humphrey were to be the welcoming committee for Kennedy. My rationale was that rather than risk a media embarrassment for the candidate, a bit of pressure by the big boys might be exerted on the local mayor and city council to work out a compromise with city employee unions on some long standing wage and benefit requests. Our union representatives had been offered a one half of one per cent salary increase.

I was a regular voter for Democratic Party candidates, but had no qualms about suggesting this tactic which was sure to attract much attention if followed up on, but my bet was that we wouldn't have to. Minnesota was to be a crucial state in the presidential election according to the gurus of that era.

The motion got a second immediately and with very little discussion or debate, passed unanimously with over five hundred employees in attendance. What followed has left me wondering a big 'what if' over all the years.

The leaders of the respective city employee unions at that time, responding to petitions calling for a special meeting, had rented a local Carpenter's Union hall for the meeting, knowing that a large crowd would be attending. They had also invited several of the area leaders of unions from private industry.

After the motion had been approved to conduct the bannering during Kennedy's visit, the chair recognized the president of the Duluth Central Labor Body, AFL-CIO, Earl Pierce. Mindful of the fact that under this guys regime we got little in the way of support for our efforts at improving our standard of living, several of us raised a point of order, objecting to a non member addressing this mass meeting. We were gaveled down by the chair.

Earl Pierce went into a diatribe about how it was completely out of order for municipal employees to be injecting themselves into the presidential election and politics and that such a display could cause Kennedy to lose the state of Minnesota and thus, the national election. He repeatedly stressed that this resolution, if not reconsidered, would be a black eye for public employees nationally.

As the maker of the approved resolution, I asked for time to rebut Mr. Pierce. I again stated that this was an attempt to get the party power brokers attention to our plight, one of the lowest paid public employee groups in Minnesota and, if this election in our state was so crucial to the national election, they, the power brokers, would find a way to convince our Democratic mayor, Mork, to settle with us. However, with respect to our 'injecting ourselves into politics', what was our miserable wage and benefit status but politics?

A few more local labor leaders also addressed the gathering and when they concluded, as if by prearranged signal, a voice in the crowd shouted a motion for reconsideration of the resolution. A quick second and a call for a vote followed.

Intimidated by the harangue from the labor leaders, the vote to reconsider won by a slim sixteen votes out of the five hundred cast. But that was sufficient. A subsequent motion to conduct bannering around city facilities, but after candidate Kennedy had departed, won approval.

On the second day of such picketing, while walking and carrying a sign on First Street in front of City Hall, I was tapped on the shoulder by someone from behind me.

"Are you Miletich?" he asked. The guy doing the asking was about six feet, one hundred ninety five pounds and looked like a fullback. He was flanked by two other guys, behemoths. Quickly, thoughts raced through my mind that someone may have hired goons to disrupt our lawful, peaceful demonstration. I rapidly looked around for fellow picketers for backup if something was about to happen.

"That's right," I answered, a bit belligerently, "who are you?

He stuck his right hand out to shake. "I'm Harvey Solon, an old buddy of your brother Steve, and I'm moving back to town from Minneapolis to take over my fathers electrical motors business, but I'm also going to promote pro wrestling in the city. Would you be interested in working ringside security for me and line up a couple of your buddies too? It is mostly to protect the wrestlers from wackos who try to get at the wrestlers or throw things."

"Sounds interesting, but do you know that we get a minimum pay for off duty extra work?" And, still suspicious, "How do you know Steve?"

"You must know that we're old friends from high school days, playing against each other."

I did. "And let me tell you a story about a troop train ride in the spring of '43.

I was a Marine on a troop train heading west toward California. Half the cars on the train contained Marines and the other half, Army. Outside Karazoza, New Mexico the train, a huge steam engine, stopped at a double tower in the desert to take on coal and water. To prevent barbs and possible friendly clashes between Marines and G.I.'s, the solders were allowed to get off to stretch their legs for a few minutes. We were scheduled to follow after they were back on board.

Naturally, we were leaning out the windows heckling the guys on the ground and they were reciprocating. Some of the G.I.'s were picking up pieces of coal and attempting to toss them into the open top of the coal tower about seventy feet above the ground, and most were missing.

One left hander was consistently tossing them in, one after another. I couldn't see his face but I knew the physique and recognized that unique left handed motion. 'Steve, Steve

*Eli J. Miletich*

Miletich' I yelled, and he turned around. I jumped through the window to the ground to a lot of hoot and hollering. We had a reunion right there in the desert."

Over the ensuing years, if I heard that story once, I heard it five hundred times.

Our friendship was cemented right then and there. Harvey introduced me to the two pro wrestlers, Larry 'The Axe' Henning and 'Handsome' Harley Race, a couple decent guys, despite the persona established for 'rassling' fans as the most vile creatures who ever jumped into the square ring.

For years, other cops like Dick Yagoda, George Kelly, Bob Kohl, Al Butler, Gene Sisto and myself worked those matches for Harvey, and he became a good friend even though his favorite jab was, "Those guys couldn't track an elephant in the snow."

---

Like the time that Gene Sisto and I were working an afternoon bit in Narco, getting ready to go relieve a team on surveillance of a couple suspects and their apartment. It was a cool November night.

We were in the downtown hillside area at about seven P.M. when a holdup call come over the police radio:

*"All squads, holdup at the Clark Gas Station, 12th Avenue east and First Street; occurred within the past four minutes, suspect wore a ski mask, is believed to be a young black male, five feet, ten inches, 160 lbs., wearing jeans and a dark blue V-neck T-Shirt and white sneakers. Suspect used a chrome plated revolver and is considered armed and dangerous. Suspect ran south on 12th toward the Plaza Shopping Center on Superior Street. Loss, around $380 in bills placed in a brown paper bag carried by the suspect."*

Several squads were closer to the scene, we were about a mile away, so we decided to check in the periphery of the Shopping Center. En route, we passed the gas station, noting four or five marked patrol units and a couple plain clothes cars, we exchanged comments that the robber was not at the crime scene any longer, and why in hell do they need that many people to interview the victim. Some of the units could be out

Eli J. Miletich

checking the area. It was a pet peeve of mine that the department had never tightened up on the practice. I remembered that years later when I could do something about it, and did so.

We proceeded south, down the block to the Plaza Shopping Center and parked in the lot which was about one block by half block in size.

I said, "How about I take Wahlgren's Drugs and you take Woolworth's and we can then take Penney's and the National Foods and the others in the strip."

The Wahlgren Store was fairly void of customers, and I stopped at the checkout counters near the front entrance and asked if any of the ladies had noticed a young black male who may have come into the store in the past several minutes, or if they happened to be looking out the huge glass windows that spanned the entire front of the store. Their response was negative.

As I turned to leave by one of the front exit doors, guess who ran right by me as I came through the door? A young black male answering the description to a capital T, but no ski mask. He was heading north toward Superior Street.

I hollered, "Stop, police!" but he appeared to accelerate without looking back. I started to run after him.

When he got to the corner of the row of shops, he turned left, west, on Superior Street with me about fifteen paces behind him. I hollered again, "Police, stop or I'll shoot." I had my gun holstered yet. He stopped dead in his tracks. Thankfully, as there was no help in sight and he had me by about twenty yards now.

"What's your name?" I demanded

"Hugh James," Was the response, with a West Indies, Jamaican, accent.

"Where are you coming from?"

"Just out jogging."

"In this weather, and dressed like that?" It was the middle of November and a small snowfall had passed through earlier in the evening leaving a light dusting of fresh white snow in the untraveled areas. It was chilly.

"I left my jacket in a friends car," he responded.

I had noticed a tan or cream colored paste smeared around his eyes, nostrils and mouth and asked him what that was. "I've got a skin condition and it's a salve for it," he replied, unconvincingly.

"You had better walk with me back to my car in the parking lot," I said, as I took him by the elbow. "You've got some explaining to do, because you match the description of a guy who just stuck up the Clark Gas Station just a block up the hill."

When we got back to the car, Gene Sisto was just emerging from the National Food Store, noticed us and walked quickly over. At that same time an old beat up Chrysler drove by two aisles to the east in the parking lot, the driver was recognized by us immediately as a young white male with a previous record of arrest and conviction for armed robbery of a corner grocery store about three years earlier.

The Chrysler continued on and parked among a row of cars about one hundred fifty feet away. The driver, obviously noting that we were standing by Hugh James, got out of his vehicle and nonchalantly walked into the National Foods Super Market.

Gene looked at me and said, "I've got to talk with somebody," and headed for the store.

In the store, Gene found John Irwin, who had quickly picked up a quart bottle of Pepsi and was standing at a checkout counter.

"What's up, John?"

"Nothing much, just wanted some pop to watch the game on TV with."

"John, do you know the young black guy we're talking with out in the parking lot?"

"Where, I didn't see you and Miletich out there?"

"I didn't say who I was with, John, you better come with me!"

Out in the parking lot, Gene walked John Irwin over to his Chrysler, shined his flashlight through the window, looked at the seats and floor. Lo and behold, there was a can of car wax on the rear floor with the cover lying alongside. The paste was a tan, creamy color. There was also a brown leather jacket lying on the back seat.

"Do you mind if I look in the inside of your car, John? asked Gene.

"Not at all, you won't find anything."

A patrol squad was just pulling alongside, having responded to a call for assistance and Gene turned Irwin over to them. "Keep and eye on him for a few minutes will you fellows."

With that, he reached into the Chrysler, took the car wax and jacket and walked over to Hugh James. With his fingers, he took a swath of paste wax from the can and held it up to James' face by his mouth and nose. A good match.

We placed James in the back seat of our vehicle and I walked to the south end of the parking lot, the direction James had come from, which was covered with melting snow and water. At the far south end was a steel guard rail protecting an incline, slight hill, sloping down to London Road.

Searching for tracks in the snow on the hill, I looked over the guard rail, saw shoe tracks leading up from London Road, and then, shining my flashlight under a small landscape type bush, saw a brown paper bag.

Climbing over the guard rail, careful not to disturb the tracks, I picked up the bag, which oddly seemed heavy for a small lunch bag, but upon opening it, found the reason why.

Inside were a chrome .32 caliber Smith-Wesson revolver and $385 in currency.

I walked back to our car, showed the findings to Gene and we placed Hugh James under arrest, followed up by walking across the lot to where John Irwin was detained and did likewise with him, both on the charge of armed robbery.

Gene had called for an Identification Tech to come to the parking lot and he took some photos of both subjects, especially close ups of Hugh James 'facial salve'. He had tried to conceal his identity with the cream colored wax, but, obviously forgot about his V-Neck T-shirt.

When the ID Tech finished those photos, I asked him to get a few shots of the footprints in the snow where the paper bag was found. He did so and, as fate would have it, a customer who had driven into the parking lot to pick up some groceries at National Foods before heading home from his office, saw us and the several police vehicles nearby, parked his car, walked over and said, "What are you guys up to?'

Gene Sisto, ever the witty one, took Harvey Solon by the elbow, walked him over to the guard rail, shined his flashlight on the footprints in the snow, explained briefly the robbery and said, "Who can't track an elephant in the snow?"

Irwin and James, interviewed separately, threw up on each other. Irwin, the driver in this instance, was to pick up James in the Plaza lot after he, James, had run a wide circle from the Clark Station. Both got two to five years in the state penitentiary.

Harvey did not change his heckling ways too much. Though he dropped the 'elephant in the snow' line for a while, it came back into his repertoire after a couple months.

## October 2

"Hello, could I speak to someone working on the case of a murdered woman found in a ditch in your city?" Asked the caller, a man who identified himself as Alfred Rosendin, a resident of southern California. It was about 6:35 P.M. and the news had just gone off the air.

"This is Lieutenant John Hall and I'm quite familiar with the case. May I help you?" Said Hall, clearly one of the most articulate, intelligent people to wear the badge in Duluth these days.

"Well," said the caller, "I'm from the San Diego area and I'm down at Lake Minnisuing closing up a friends cabin for the winter. I drove here, and I might have some information which may help. At least I hope it does. It involves a guy driving a dark blue Toyota Wagon with Colorado plates who I met in Fort Morgan and drove along with him to Wisconsin."

Hall quickly asked for the man's name, his present location as well as his permanent address and phone number, then offered to drive to Lake Minnisuing, about thirty five miles to the south in Wisconsin, to interview him.

"No, that won't be necessary, I've got a lot of time on my hands and I won't mind driving to Duluth to talk with you, I hear that most of the city is on a hillside and the lights are spectacular at night, so I'd like to see your town. Just give me directions to police headquarters once I cross the river that lies between Minnesota and Wisconsin."

Hall gave him directions, hoping the guy wasn't a crackpot. He also wondered if he should call the Douglas County Sheriff's Department, across the bay, and have them go check out the location on that lake and see if the caller was indeed there.

"I'm leaving right now. I started my car to warm it up for the drive since I thought you would want a statement from me." Said Rosendin, who then closed off the conversation and hung up.

Hall immediately called Pat Alexander at home, wondering if the caller was for real.

"Hey, John, you're up to date on this case, would you mind talking to the guy, get a complete statement, as best as he can remember. You might want to have another officer in there with you sharing note taking while the tape recorder is getting it also. That should cover all bases. I'd sure like to come down there, but I just sat down to supper and then I want to catch some winks. Its been fourteen and fifteen hour shifts since this thing started," Pleaded Alexander.

"No problem," said Hall, Bev is working days and is ready to go home, but I'm sure she will be glad to stay over and give a hand."

Beverly Ecklund, also a Lieutenant in the Detective Bureau, is one cop who will give assistance when needed, not hesitating to get down in the trenches.

Alexander sat thinking after cradling the phone. Things couldn't be working out better. This guy could turn out to be an important witness, maybe a key witness, and we've got two of the brightest most tenacious, streetwise supervisors to interview him.

Hall and Ecklund, both promoted to Lieutenant on the same day by me, had always had been involved in a friendly rivalry. When the results of the Civil Service promotional test for

Lieutenant had been posted earlier that year, there was a small fraction of a percent separating their respective scores. When vacancies subsequently occurred, as had been expected due to retirements, both had paid me a visit to assure themselves that I would not be passing over any eligibles, such as themselves, over some long forgotten difference of opinion, such differences of opinion not uncommon to cops who are striving to do their job well.

When Alfred Rosendin arrived thirty seven minutes after he had called, Hall and Ecklund were waiting with a stenographer and tape recorder. This guy has got to be pretty serious, thought Hall, reminding himself of the distance and traffic he would have encountered making the trip from the lake, along with the many signal lights and stop signs he would have hit once he came into Superior, Wisconsin across the bay.

"I'm a contractor," said the southern Californian, " and one of my good friends, Dr. Suhada Russi, owns this cabin on Lake Minnisuing which he and his family try to use most of July and part of August. They have relatives and friends who use the place once in a while when the doctors family is not there, too."

"The doctor usually comes up in late September, does a little bird hunting for a week or so, then closes up the cabin for the winter."

Closing a cabin, a seasonal home away from home in the northern tier of states, means shutting off the water supply at the well pump, draining the water lines, flushing all other lines, including the toilet tank and bowl and securing all windows and doors, generally making the building weather proof. Lake Minnisuing is one of the thousands of lakes in northern Wisconsin, as well as Minnesota with cabins dotting the shoreline and it is not unusual to see license plates from around the country in their driveways.

"This year it became an impossibility because of a heavy case load, so he asked me. This is kind of a slack time of year for me, so it worked out fine. We're friends, but of course, I'm also a businessman, so there's naturally a monetary consideration involved, and it is a nice break for me to see a part of the country I'm not familiar with."

"The doctor is originally from Armenia, but he has adapted well to the American culture, mores and idiosyncrasies."

This guy speaks well for a contractor, mused Bev Ecklund.

"The doctor is a plastic surgeon and he says that there's almost an epidemic of people who want to look like something other than their original selves, so he's accommodating them. That's why I'm here."

Hall interjected politely, "Now, you indicated that you may have some important information for us, can you explain what that is and, if you don't mind, start from the beginning, much the same as if you were telling a story to your wife or some friends. We'll just let you continue, but if something you say strikes a chord with one of us we may interject to ask a question or two, but try to keep your train of thought. Okay?"

"Yes," said Rosendin, "And I hope this is not a waste of your time."

"I have a strong hunch it won't be,"said Bev Ecklund, "But please go on."

"Well, Doctor Russi gave me directions, the Interstates', U.S. Highways and so forth, on how to get to northern Wisconsin, even places to gas up. He's made the trip dozens of times, though he flies more often than not."

"On the evening of September 29th, I stopped for gas in Fort Morgan, Colorado.

It was a self service and, while I was pumping gas, the man across the island from me started to chat. A young guy, between twenty five and thirty, I'd guess. He seemed like a personable kind. We talked about the upcoming World Series. I left after I filled up, getting back to the Interstate.

About three and one half hours later, we met again at a truck stop outside Lincoln, Nebraska. I had already gassed up, and was in the coffee shop when he walked in. I invited him to sit and have his coffee with me. He said his name was Mike.

He told me he was a seaman and was heading for the East Coast to catch on with a freighter, but he was in no particular hurry.

Back at the gas station in Fort Morgan I had noticed what looked like several weeks of rumpled up clothing and a blanket piled up in the back of the station wagon he was driving. Lot of clothes washing this guy faces, I had thought to myself.

I told him where I was heading and what I was going to do, and suggested that if he was in no real hurry, I could offer him a

185

job, helping me, for a few days. No great pay, but meals would be included. And when the cabin was closed up and property cleaned and straightened around, he could resume his trip by just hopping on Interstate 94 and heading directly east.

He said, 'Great, this will help me with gas money.'

We then drove in tandem to northern Wisconsin, stopping along the way for the necessary gas and lunch breaks. Oh, I don't know if I had mentioned it before or not, but Mike was driving a dark blue Toyota Station Wagon, with Colorado license plates.

We arrived at the cabin at about mid afternoon on September 30th. After relaxing for a bit with a beer, we went right to work and pulled in the dock which was still in the water. You know you have to get docks out of the water around here before the lakes freeze up. We anchored it to a couple large trees with a good, strong chain, placed a heavy duty lock on that chain and called it a day. I had the next days activities all laid out in an outline Suhada Russi had given to me.

I was pretty darned tired after all that driving and then taking that dock out of the water, so I looked in the phone book, found a neat restaurant listed in the Yellow pages which specialized in ribs. It was in a town called Solon Springs, only about fifteen minutes away, so I called, ordered enough for two and drove in and picked the order up. Mike went with me.

After we finished, he said he needed some smokes and was going to look around this fabulous resort country for a short while, and he was sure that because I was so tired that I wanted to hit the hay and get a good nights rest.

He was right. He left at about 7:15 P.M. I do remember thinking what in hell is he going to see in the way of resorts and cabins when the sun had just about set and night was coming in fast?

He got back about 9:30 P.M. and went into the other bedroom without saying anything.

The next day, October 1st, we got up fairly early and tended to the chores and got a lot or work done. I'll say this for him, he's not the strongest or stoutest looking person in appearance, but he worked like a beaver. I was glad that I had asked him if he wanted to work for a couple days. It was actually cutting my work by more than half.

Anyway, once, as I passed by his Toyota Wagon, I happened to look in the back again and noticed that it did not look so messy and things were arranged in some semblance of order, and the clothes were folded and stacked up.

I didn't think anything about it then, except that maybe he stopped by a trash receptacle and threw some of his litter away.

That evening the TV news carried the story about the discovery of the woman's body in your city with no apparent identification. We talked about how terrible that was and how it was not fair to her family if they, the police, never find out who she is.

For dinner, we barbecued a couple nice sirloins I had picked up the night before in Solon Springs. After, Mike stepped out on the porch, saying he was going to have a cigarette and catch some of the cool, crisp air of the northland. In about ten minutes I heard him drive off and thought he was just going for another ride. He didn't return that night or the next day.

In the morning I didn't make any connection between your situation and this guy Mike and I still had a number of things to do before my job was complete, so I went about my chores. I finished them this morning, still ahead of schedule, so I was going to spend the next couple days bird hunting. Yes, I picked up a Wisconsin bird license this afternoon.

It wasn't until I saw the news tonight that I realized that Mike, or whoever he is, could be involved. It was then that I got nervous, no, correct that, I was scared shitless. I locked the doors and checked out the interior of the cabin.

I had the only key. He never did bring any luggage into the cabin, only bringing in his shaving kit in the morning, and returning it to his wagon when he was done cleaning up. I had thought that being a drifter of sorts this was the way he usually traveled.

As I was looking over the cabin, I noted that several small items were missing, especially Suhada Russi's credit cards. The doctor keeps four major company credit cards at the cabin for use when he's staying here. He keeps them on the fireplace mantel.That brings me up to the present, when I called you as soon as the news was over."

Bev Ecklund, thinking ahead, said, "Mr. Rosendin, we believe you may have helped us immensely. I wish all our witnesses were as thorough in recalling details as you have been. Now, you said that you planned to bird hunt for a few days before driving back to California. That's good! We're going to try to line up a sketch artist who might be able to do a drawing of Mike according to the description you provide. You were in his company for over two days, do you think you can remember and describe him to us?"

"I"m, pretty sure I can, and if you need me to be around a few days in addition to what I had planned, no problem. I'll just call my wife and let her know what I'm up to. She can call the doctor and let him know what he's got me into. I'll have her tell him about his credit cards, too."

"Just a couple more things," said John Hall." "Do you know if the man who said his name was Mike was seen by anyone else? I mean, are there any nearby cabin residents who may have seen him when you guys were moving around the property, pulling the dock out of the water, piling up the lawn furniture and so forth."

"Matter of fact there's a neighbor on the left side who came over and introduced himself and asked us who we were and put me through a third degree. I guess that he wanted to be sure we were not some burglars who would come back after dark and rip off everything of value. I showed him the letter of authorization which Dr. Russi had given me, and a photocopy of the doctors license to practice medicine in California. That satisfied him. There was a couple on the other side who waved and shouted hello. I know that they also got a good look at the both of us."

"Good," said Hall. "We're going to try to talk to them. And before we finish for tonight, can you give us a description of Mike, as best as you can recall, age, height, weight, color of hair, color of eyes, length and style of hair, facial appearance, clothes he was wearing, jacket, if you saw one, hats he might have worn, visible scars, and so on."

Again, Rosendin displayed a good memory. "He's a white male, between twenty five and thirty years of age, about five feet, nine inches tall, one hundred sixty five to one hundred seventy pounds. He has an oval face with a brown droopy mustache and several days growth of beard, long scraggly brown hair, shoulder length, and brown eyes which are narrow and squinty."

"How about clothing?" Bev Ecklund asked.

Without hesitating, Rosendin replied, "He was wearing the same jeans the whole time he was with me, a light blue western style shirt and dirty old white sneakers. Now, what he had in the back of that Toyota, I'm not sure. He wore a dark blue nylon windbreaker jacket toward evening when it would start to cool off, but he usually kept that in the wagon when he wasn't wearing it. That's about it. If I think of anything else, I'll make a note of it to be sure I bring it up to you."

"Mr. Rosendin, you have been a great help toward putting this puzzle together, if this guy is out there, we stand a much better chance of locating him because of what you have told us." Hall said. "Here are our cards, and I'll write the name of Detective Sergeant Patrick Alexander on the back of my card for you. He's the officer coordinating the investigation. Can you call him first thing tomorrow? Try to get a good nights sleep, because I'm sure tomorrow is going to be a busy day for you."

"By the way, we are going to contact the Douglas County Sheriff's Department, that's the jurisdiction the cabin is in, and ask them to check around the place as frequently as possible through the night. Okay? My guess is that he's clear out of this area, but we want to be sure."

Rosendin seemed relieved, said thank you, and left.

Hall, as promised, called the Douglas County Sheriff's in Wisconsin, talked to a sergeant, and gave him an overview of the situation. Cooperation, as always practiced between law enforcement agencies in this area, was assured.

———————————

By now, I was called by Alexander at home and given an update, I had issued a directive to all involved in the investigation that the county attorneys office was only to be given the preliminary reports reference the finding of the victim and the information about the vehicle. No need for prosecuting attorneys to botch this with a press conference,. That office was headed by a politician who claimed to be apolitical. Duluth has always had a high ratio of citizen participation in politics and for a politician to claim to be apolitical is hypocritical.

## Chapter Fourteen

## October 3

About mid morning on October 3rd, Alfred Rosendin came in to Police Headquarters to meet with Pat Alexander and Detective Sergeant Harry Abrams, who was going to assist in following up on the interview of the previous evening.

Alexander introduced himself and Abrams to Rosendin and immediately proceeded.

"Mr. Rosendin, we have a member of the City Graphics Department waiting to attempt a sketch of this Mike fellow from the description you may provide to her. She has never performed this function as she works with business developers and engineers, but she is one heck of an artist in her own right. She is highly thought of among her peers. We don't have a police sketch artist available in the whole area, so we have decided to give this an attempt." said Alexander, "Is that okay with you?"

"That's no problem with me, I understand that time is of essence in a matter like this, I just hope that I can give a clear enough description," answered Rosendin.

Sergeant Abrams then brought in Dawn Kast, Engineer Division Graphics Coordinator for the City of Duluth. Her endeavors had never remotely been associated with those of law enforcement. Rather, her line of work was of a less delicate nature than crime, working with engineers, but she was game to give this project a try.

With the verbal description provided by Rosendin, Dawn Kast utilized some mechanical composites furnished by Sergeant John Kalenowski and did a rough draft of the suspect. It was good, and with more detail provided by Rosendin, it turned out a near masterpiece.

That morning Pat Alexander had also called Dr. Suhada Russi's two neighbors at the lake cabin and just before noon they came to the Detective Bureau and added a touch here and there. Alexander suggested some color be added, and when Dawn Kast finished her work, it was almost photographic in appearance. Rosendin looked and approved.

Alexander then asked Lieutenant Donneta Wickstrom to take the sketch to the photo lab where dozens of copies were made, then oversaw the dissemination of the sketch to area law enforcement agencies.

Bob Harvey, Special Agent in Charge of the Duluth FBI office, saw to the distribution through that federal agency's network to the entire Midwest.

We weren't going to celebrate with beer and wine just yet!

---

In the afternoon of the same day, the father and brother of the victim arrived at the Duluth International Airport aboard a Northwest 727.

Bartholomew Voorsanger had met his son, Matthew and Matthew's fiancee, at the Minneapolis-St. Paul Airport, and they continued their sad journey to Duluth together. Alexander and another skilled investigator, Lieutenant Donneta Wickstrom, were on hand to guide them through their ordeal.

After they all exchanged introductions, Alexander invited the group to coffee in an airport restaurant. There, he patiently and quietly explained what the police knew; how the body had been found, that they needed positive identification if in fact the victim was Roxanna. He gently warned them that she was badly injured and disfigured by the beating. He asked if they would feel up to viewing the body now, and they said yes.

While driving from the airport, Lieutenant Wickstrom and Alexander engaged the Voorsangers in conversation where they gleaned a whole lot of background on Roxanna.

Bartholomew Voorsanger offered that "As a child in Iran, Roxanna was adopted by us and brought back to the States to be raised as a member of our family." And he continued in a manner that was neither pretentious or condescending, describing the upper middle class life in suburban Connecticut. "The family, including all the relatives, doted on her from day one, and when Matthew was born five years later, they both continued receiving equal affection from us, their parents. Life was relaxed and pleasant for the family."

"In her early twenties Roxanna met and soon married the man of her dreams, went west with him, had a son who is now five years old. They divorced after seven years of marriage.

*Eli J. Miletich*

"Lately, she was earning her living as a seamstress, and a darn good one at that but she was attending classes, studying to be a hair stylist."

"Though she loved both her mother, brother and me, she was proud of her independence. She politely, but firmly, declined our many invitations to move back with us until she could complete her training and get her feet back on the ground again." Voorsanger paused, and it was obvious to Wickstrom and Alexander that he was about to become emotional, so they suggested stopping at Police Headquarters first to look at photos of the victim, their intent being to soften the impact of looking at her body later, rather that stopping at the mortuary first.

Mr. Voorsanger was later to recall that experience in a letter to the Duluth News Tribune. The city's only daily; the Tribune is a throwback to the days of the Old West, where the town's newspaper publisher wielded far too much influence for a rag staffed by editors and writers of questionable qualifications and character. Voorsanger's letter was never published, for whatever editorial reason, here's what he wrote, in part:

198

*This letter wishes to honor Sergeants Patrick Alexander and Lieutenant Donneta Wickstrom of the Duluth Police force.*

*A phone call from Sergeant Alexander to my Manhattan office on an early October evening started the searing journey. My daughter had been missing from her Boulder home for five days and Alexander quietly explained they believed my daughter's body had been found alongside a road near the Duluth Airport.*

*Would I come to Duluth the next day for an identification?*

*" After being met at the airport by Sergeant Alexander, we drove to the downtown area. We arrived at police headquarters, stowing our bags. Gently, Sergeant Alexander explained the identification procedure may be difficult, she might not be my daughter and the true identification not conclusive, since she was disfigured. He then pulled out four Polaroid to prepare us. My ability to focus was difficult, but my son Matthew said 'yes, positively, that was Roxanna.' I could not be sure because she was so badly injured. Matthew is a medical student, so I trusted his judgment. Privately, I knew she was dead.*

*Lieutenant Wickstrom then suggested that we go to the mortuary.*

*As we drove, my thoughts were of the horror committed upon my daughter. To even the most jaded of New Yorkers, the events which have been unfolding could only be a sordid nightmare, let alone take place in an alien, unknown city in Minnesota. How did her body travel 1,000 miles to Minnesota? What happened?*

*We arrived at a residence near the lake, apparently an old stately home which had been renovated and converted to a mortuary. Matthew and I were guided to the viewing room which was bathed in baby blue light, royal blue in color, her body raised on a table, covered and bandaged.*

*Yes, it was Roxanna, she was dead. It was unbearable, she seemed so angry, so defenseless, yet so silent. The worst experience of my life was to view the battered body of my dead child. I cried and cried, the reality of her departure now too vivid to deny. I spent the final moments with her alone.*

*Sergeant Alexander quietly escorted us out and explained gently they would need statements from us. Who was she? Her*

200

*friends? What type of person? Where could contacts be made? In silence we arrived at police headquarters and were interviewed by Lieutenant Wickstrom.*

*As we departed the police department, Alexander told me headquarters had started searching for her stolen station wagon, information was being wired across the country, the FBI contacted and information sent to the local media and newspapers. He was clearly soft spoken but powerfully in charge."*

That the Tribune never published Voorsangers letter is for them to answer. Let three, five, seven, nine or more radicals demonstrate on the steps of City Hall or have an individual make charges of police use of excessive force, and it's a running front page story for weeks. If the truth be told they, the editors and publishers, have always had to swallow hard to print a favorable story about local police work.

*Eli J. Miletich*

## Chapter Fifteen

When reflecting on my career as a cop, particularly those days in investigations, it stirs up many fond memories of the people I've worked with and the cases that we handled as a team. My memory bank rings clear with the words of our boss for many years, Detective Inspector Russ Barber, "By the way, you don't have too much success in law enforcement unless you work as a team."

Many instances come to mind, but an outstanding case was one involving an escapee from the state prison at Stillwater. The city by that name, located on the St. Croix River, is host to one of the largest prisons in the Midwest housing felons. It lies near the Wisconsin state line, about thirty miles east of the Twin Cities of St. Paul and Minneapolis.

Actually he didn't escape from the state pen. Rather, he was in a county jail facility in Carver County, near Stillwater, awaiting trial for a homicide allegedly committed in the prison, when he broke loose. All law enforcement agencies in the upper Midwest had been notified of his escape.

202

On a particularly quiet afternoon in the Narco Unit, I received a call from a long time confidential informant whom I can only describe as number 32 as to do otherwise would certainly place that informants life in danger.

"Eli, would you guys be interested in the whereabouts of the escapee from Stillwater, Gary Goodwin."

I chuckled, "Yeah, and so would every cop in a ten state area."

"I'm not kidding, I'm serious, he's here in Duluth. I saw him last night."

"You're not kidding?"

"Hell no, I told you, I saw him last night and he has been staying with a relative of a good friend of mine for the past two nights. He says that when he escaped from the Carver County Jail he stole a deputy's marked car and drove to downtown Minneapolis. He then hid the car in an old abandoned warehouse in the riverfront area.

"He walked back downtown and, around Washington Avenue and Third Street, then forced his way into the unlocked door of a car waiting at a red signal light. It was driven by an elderly man who had his wife as a passenger. Goodwin put the deputy's gun to the old guys head and forced them to go to their home where he held them hostage for three days.

He got a ride from Minneapolis to Duluth with a friend and he's been staying at this apartment in the West End since then."

I asked, "Okay, where is he at?"

"Not so fast." said number 32.

"I'm scheduled to go to court next Thursday on a drunk driving charge. Can you see if it can be dismissed. If you can do that, then you will get his location. Otherwise, I'm not taking a chance, you know this guy already has two convictions for murder, don't you?"

"No, as a matter of fact, I don't know anything about him other than what is on the bulletin announcing his escape. It says that he was going to trial next week for the alleged murder of a fellow inmate," I said. It was true, the information we had on him was very scanty.

32 laughed, "You cops don't have a network as good as the street people and the cons have. He was in Stillwater because

he killed a guy while at St. Cloud, and he was in St. Cloud because he killed a guy in civilian life. All the murders were by garroting.

St. Cloud is a state penal institution for so called youthful offenders, ages eighteen through twenty five.

"Goodwin was transferred to Carver County Jail for his own safety because rumors had it that other convicts were about to off him."

Amazing, the informant knew all this. We didn't!

"Tell you what," I said, "give me twenty minutes to check out your drunk driving charge. I'll need to talk to the officers who made the arrest and the Traffic Inspector as well as the judge who will be on the bench. I can't guarantee anything, you know, but call me back in exactly twenty minutes. I'll have to see if what you say about this guy is factual too. Who are the officers who busted you?"

"The two cops are Sinnott and Hansen, both usually okay guys, but this time they were really pricks," he insisted.

"But you weren't, I'm sure. Call me back in twenty."

*Eli J. Miletich*

First, I checked with the officers. both were off duty and at home, as they were on the night shift that week, so I took the chance that they had already slept their five or six hours before getting ready for the next shift. They were sleeping, but their wives woke them.

Fortunately both Joe Sinnott and Pete Hansen are street wise cops and, when I explained the potential for apprehending the escapee, they readily agreed. I assured them that there would be no deal if we did not get Goodwin.

Next I went to the office of Traffic Inspector Ray Peplinski.

"You know, Sergeant, I don't like letting people off for serious traffic offenses, but this sounds like trading an old beat up Chevvy for a new Cadillac. Okay with me, and as you say, with Sinnott and Hansen, but you are going to have to talk with Judge Tom Bujold, as he is on the Traffic Court bench next Thursday."

"Sure am, and I also need to check out the info on why this guy was in prison in the first place," I offered.

Municipal Court was on third floor in City Hall and I quickly found out that Judge Bujold was indeed scheduled to be hearing traffic cases the next week.

"Where's Judge Bujold now?" I asked Clerk of Court Arne Johnson, an old friend from high school days. We had played on Denfeld High football teams together. He was presently doing a lot of officiating for high school and college games.

"In his courtroom, conducting a preliminary hearing on a rape case. I don't think you want to interrupt him unless it's really important," cautioned Arne.

"It is," I said as I stepped into the courtroom and walked forward to the bench.

One of the attorneys was speaking to the judge as I came up to his right side.

The judge looked up from his note taking, "What is going on, Sergeant?"

"Judge, may I see you for a few minutes in your chambers? It's very important."

"It had better be," He said and announced a short recess in the hearing.

In chambers I explained the situation to Judge Tom Bujold, a stern guy in his courtroom, but off the bench he had a great sense of humor.

"I never knew that this character was an informant of yours. Can't you do something to keep this person out of trouble. Seems like there's a courtroom appearance at least once a month. You believe this Goodwin guy is in town, huh?"

"We'll have to wait and see. If we don't get him, there is no deal with the informant, and that is clearly understood," I answered.

"Fine, go ahead then, we'll probably see that character in court again in a month or so."

"Thanks Judge, if this works out all right you will probably have the escapee in front of you tomorrow morning."

I got back down to my desk with a couple minutes to spare before number 32 was to call and it gave me time to call Floyd Bowman of the Minnesota Bureau of Criminal Apprehension, a retired Duluth cop, now working for the state as an investigator.

Quickly, I explained to him what I had, and he confirmed the two previous homicides by Goodwin and the pending trial for the third. "He used a thin wire for the garroting in all three instances.," Bowman pointed out, " and, you might want to tell your informant that there is a reward being offered for this guys arrest. The State Corrections Board has posted five hundred bucks and I'm pretty sure that the Crime Bureau will come up with a couple hundred too."

I asked him if he wanted in on our manhunt and he said he would be right over. His office was only ten minutes away.

Next, I went into my boss's office and laid out the scenario to Russ Barber. He was a guy who didn't need to have things explained to him twice, and when I finished he said, "We're going to need a lot of help on this. If this information is correct we know that Goodwin has at least one weapon, the .357 that he took from the Deputy Jailer when he escaped by beating him up. How can I be of help?"

"Inspector, I'm glad you asked that question. I think we need your expertise in setting up a surveillance on the apartment building the guy is in, and for directing the move we make on the place when we find out that he is in fact there. Number 32 is going to be calling me back in about thirty seconds if my watch is correct. I'll be back when I finish talking to him."

"In the meantime, I will start putting together a list of people we can use on the operation. Depending where he is, we should figure on at least ten people," volunteered Barber. With him directing this, there would be no problem drawing officers from the various units. Then he added, "Let's not do anything with the County Attorney's office on this yet, until, and if, we get this guy. I don't want those guys to screw it up!"

I got back to my desk still laughing about Barbers crack just as the phone rang.

"Right on the second, ain't I?" It was number 32. "Have you got anything for me?"

I told 32 we had a deal. "Now, do you have anything for us. Remember, there's no deal if we don't get Goodwin, so you had better be right."

"He's at 1925 West 3rd Street, in the West End. There's six apartments in that building and he's in the one on the second floor, in the left rear. The apartment is rented by a woman who is related to a friend of mine. She's Native American. He's part Native American."

"Yeah, we are aware of his ethnic background. We do need a good description of him as you saw him last night. The color of shirt and pants, color and length of hair and kind of shoes he's wearing."

"He's wearing a red and black checked shirt, black jeans, cowboy boots and a Twins baseball hat. He has long black hair, tied in a pony tail in back. He is about 5 feet eight inches tall, about one hundred fifty pounds."

"Are you sure that he's still at the apartment?"

"I think so, he was saying that he was going to move to another location tonight, after it gets dark," answered 32.

I thought I'd let 32 know that there may be another incentive to be accurate in this information. "The state is offering up to five hundred if he's captured. So in addition to having your driving charge dismissed, you will do all right in cash."

"Great, I can use some cash about now," 32 exclaimed. "There's another thing you should know. That building has several other Native American families living in it and they have young sons. I counted five young guys with pony tails coming and going from the building last night. And, if they have buddies, you could have a problem."

"Thanks pal. Where are you going to be later on in case I want to talk to you?"

"I'll be at the Pub Bar."

"Good, hang tight, and thanks." I hung up.

I returned to Inspector Barbers office and he went over a list of personnel he had designated to serve on the team which would set up surveillance on the building until we were ready to go. I told him that Floyd Bowman had volunteered and Barber added his name. Several years before, when he had locked in his pension with our department at twenty five years of service he, Bowman, had accepted a position with the State Crime Bureau and was assigned to the northeastern corner of the state. He didn't have to move.

Additionally, Ron Swanson of the Drug Enforcement Agency who was working on a separate case with one of our Narco Unit's guys had offered to help.

I let the Inspector know of the fact there were an undetermined number of young Native American males living on the premises, not counting some who just came to visit, all possibly wearing a pony tail.

"We will just have to be very extra careful and be sure we have the right guy when we make our move. We don't want any civil rights law suit. Let's go back to the Squad Room, I've got all the people who will be working on this waiting to be briefed," said the Inspector.

Assignments were made. Positions from which all doors and windows to the building could be seen were determined. Officers were to go to nearby buildings which offered the best view, identify themselves to the occupants and ask to use their home for an observation point, but not explain what it was they were looking at specifically.

Three officers were detailed to remain in vehicles a safe distance from the apartment building and were to be dispatched to follow any male who resembled the escapee to whatever his destination.

No move to take the subject was to be made until we had determined that he was still at 1925 West 3rd and only when Inspector Barber gave the word. "And, by the way," Russ Barber said, "even though this man is a convicted murderer, we do not use deadly force unless the situation calls for it.

The man is a member of a minority, and I don't want any racial claims either. After he is taken into custody, Sergeants Dwyer and Otto will be the transporting squad."

All went to their assigned places. Because most of our unmarked, plain, cars are known to the bad guys, I was to utilize my own private vehicle for an occasional pass by the residence, and to stay loose in case it was necessary to contact the informant, as well as to provide some direction for the people on surveillance.

It started to drizzle, then rain harder, making it tough for the surveillance people to see clearly at times. This difficulty was enhanced on several occasions when a young Native American male was seen to be leaving the building, but after close inspection by one of the mobile roving units, he was cleared.

At about two and one half hours into the operation, a Yellow Cab was observed to pull up in front of the apartment building. After a couple minutes, a young man came out of the building carrying two paper bags and got into the cab.

One of the surveillance vehicles was sent to conduct a loose tail. The officer reported that the passenger was dropped off at 14 Piedmont Avenue, only about seven blocks away.

I contacted the cab company dispatcher and asked him to send that cab to police headquarters to see Inspector Barber. The Inspector wanted to debrief him to help determine if that was our man.

I went to the nearest outdoor pay phone and called number 32 at the Pub Bar.

"We think he went to another house, but we want to be sure. Can you check to see if he's still there?" I asked.

"Geez, I don't know, they might think something is fishy."

"Get your buddy to take you there on some pretense that he needs to see his relative about."

"Okay, I'll call you back in one half hour," 32 said and hung up after I gave him the number of the phone I would be standing by.

In about fifteen minutes our surveillance teams were reporting two escapee look a likes, with a female, showing up at 1925 West 3rd in a van. I knew who it was and interceded by advising them that I was acquainted with the parties and that they shared an apartment in that building. Don't reveal your informants to anyone but your close partners!

The two young men and the female from the van, left the building after about five minutes. I stepped back into the phone booth. The phone rang in another five minutes.

"You're right, he's gone. He's at 14 Piedmont Avenue with another friend of his. The guy knows he can be violent but, because he fears for his life,he agreed to put him up. I don't know whether it's an upstairs apartment or down. Gary told him that he was leaving town tomorrow night. Gotta go,I'm being watched."

I passed the word to the surveillance crew and then met with Russ Barber who had hopped into a car when he heard me telling the team to take up new positions near the Piedmont Avenue location.

"I think we should go in just as soon as it gets a little darker. Any problems with that? That way we might be able to move in close enough without being seen from inside the apartment." That was the old master talking.

"Great, Inspector, there's two apartments, up and down, in that building, and we don't know which one our man is in. I'd suggest that we try the downstairs first, because there is a foyer entry. I've been in that building several times in recent years, and if we hit the wrong one, we should be able to recover quick and run up the stairs. On the other hand, if we go upstairs first and it's wrong, we will have made too much noise and alerted them."

"Okay, let's get about a half dozen of the team to meet us in that parking lot around the corner from the Ryland Ford building where we won't be seen, and move from there."

From the parking lot we went quietly, single file and at intervals, to the front stairs of the building and up the stairs.

I tried the main entry door. It was unlocked. I waited in the foyer until all six officers and Inspector Barber were in.

Very quietly, I tried the handle to the first floor apartment and when there was a little resistance, I gave a shove and it popped open. We rushed in and I ran toward the rear of the place.

When I reached the kitchen I knew immediately that we were in the wrong unit. Sitting at the kitchen table, eating something, soup or beans out of a can, was a very elderly Native American couple. One seventy five watt bulb glowed from a single wire on which it was suspended from the ceiling.

Recovering quickly, I then ran past the other officers who had rushed in after me, into the hallway and up the stairs.

When I got to the landing at the top, I saw that the door to the apartment was fully open but it was almost pitch black inside, except for a faint light coming in through a living room window from the corner street light outside.

It was then that I saw a silhouette of a figure running from that front room toward the back. I ran after that figure, through the dining room and into what I could tell, by the odor, was the kitchen.

Halfway into the room, I bumped into something and quickly grabbed the pair of arms of someone sitting in a chair. I squeezed as hard as I could shouting, 'Police, don't move.'

Just then, I heard the sound of rustling paper coming from the floor behind me. All of a sudden, someone else ran into the kitchen and I heard the voice of one of the Narco-Vice Unit officers, Rod Radich, holler, "Don't move that hand further."

Almost at the same time, Sergeant Jim Otto ran in and turned on the light. I was holding on to the tenant of the apartment. Rod Radich was holding his .38 caliber service revolver in Gary Goodwins ear. Goodwin was lying on the floor beside a small bed, holding on to a brown paper bag. An examination of the content of the bag revealed the service revolver, a .357 Magnum which he, Goodwin, had taken from the Carver County Deputy when he beat him and escaped.

Gary Goodwin was transported to St. Louis County Jail by Sergeants Jim Otto and Dick Dwyer.

*Eli J. Miletich*

The follow up investigation revealed that the tenant had allowed Goodwin to stay at his apartment out of fear for his life and he was not charged.

Before we cleared from the building Inspector Barber and I went back down to the apartment of the elderly couple and apologized for busting in on them. They were very stoical about it. We also advised them that we would be leaving a report for the City Attorney's office, in particular the Claims Investigator, and we encouraged them to file a claim if they felt it necessary to do do.

Later, at headquarters, when preparing reports, I got a call from #32. "Did you get him?"

"Yes, and much thanks to you. Count on your DWI being dropped."

"How about my money, we had to borrow a couple bucks, actually $3.75, as a cover story as my excuse for going back to the apartment."

Since making the arrest, we had found out that the state Crime Bureau was also upping the reward ante by three hundred dollars, and our own department added another two hundred. So with the five bills from the Corrections Department, the total came to one thousand. However, before telling 32 about that, I decided do have a little fun, so I said, "No problem, we'll refund you the $3.75 so you can pay the woman back."

"Big fuckin' spender!" was the reply.

Not wanting to lose a prized informant, I then detailed the reward money and you could hear the sigh of relief over the phone. "And, don't forget, that court date has been eliminated, so you now have a chance to straighten out your life."

The next day when arraigned before Judge Bujold, Goodwin, without hesitation, acknowledged that he "was going to shoot that first cop who ran into the kitchen, if I could have got to the gun before that other cop came in."

I was sitting at my desk that next morning compiling reports when Fred McDougall came in. Fred was the Indian Ombudsman for the State of Minnesota and a long time friend.

"Good morning, Fred, What brings you out and about so early in the morning?"

"Hi Eli, I got a call from the guy you guys arrested last night. Says that a couple of your guys abused him on the way to the jail last night. Called him a dirty Indian and a few other inflammatory, discriminatory remarks. You know, it's my job to look into those kinds of allegations."

"Fred, we almost anticipated this kind of bullshit so Inspector Barber made sure that the transporting officers would be Sergeants Otto and Dwyer. Does that say anything?"

Fred, being part Native American knew the two officers and that they were also proud of their part Native American heritage, and that they would never engage in such behavior.

"Well, I am going to the County Jail to talk with him, but it looks like it will be a short conversation." When completed, Fred dropped by again to let me know that the conversation was indeed short. That was the end of that.

A postscript to this case is that Goodwin served less than ten years for his offenses, i.e., three murders in addition to the deputy badly beaten and escape from custody. He was released on parole and returned back to his old haunts and buddies.

Intelligence reports kept coming in that he was involved with a burglary and stickup ring. In the early nineties, he was arrested and convicted in Superior, Wisconsin, for the armed robbery of a bar, and it's patrons, whereby he took a few shots at the floor and ceiling while pulling the robbery, in an act intended to intimidate his victims. He got ten years for that, and Wisconsin, unlike Minnesota, assures the public that he serves most of that time.

## Chapter Sixteen

In the Narco-Vice office the atmosphere was pretty relaxed during my term there, except when getting ready for a search or a bust of a suspect. The guys all understood that the nature of the work, dealing with dopers, pimps, prostitutes and some of the other dregs of the community as well as informants and even complainants, was stressful enough, so we tried to talk about our families and kid around a lot. I encouraged that, always saying, "When the bell rings, though, let's be ready to give 110%." Occasionally, when I noticed that something was not being handled right or that things had grown a bit too lax, we had a sort of closed door session, with me slamming the office door behind me when entering for dramatic effect. The guys got to calling it the 'slammed door chewing out".

In another incident involving good fortune, and old friend Harvey Solon, something that actually started off on a Saturday night, we got involved even though it did not have anything to do with drugs, pimps or prostitutes.

Carol, my wife, and I were guests at a wine tasting party hosted by Harvey in the party room of the condo where his apartment was. I had never been to a wine tasting party and what I presumed might be a stuffy party of a group of his business associates and old friends did not particularly excite me.

Instead, his guests, included business associates as well as old friends and some of his boyhood buddies, Judges Don Odden, Jack Litman and Luther Eckman.

They, the judges, also were part of an every other week lunch group which included TV sportscaster Marsh Nelson and Tribune sports writer Bruce Bennett. Those lunches were always hilarious in that Harvey was better than Don Rickles with his wisecracks and barbs. Example: If someone would stop at our table to greet Harvey but did not know the rest of us, Harvey would introduce Judge Odden by name, then add, "the best judge.... (pause) that money can buy." The other judges, Litman and Eckman, were not immune either. Likewise, Sisto and me with the "can't track an elephant in the snow", bit.

Harvey, divorced, was living in the Miller Hill Manor, a security condominium with many of the perks associated with condo living, a huge indoor pool, sauna, fitness center, two banquet, party, rooms.

It was in the banquet rooms that the wine tasting party was held. Harvey spared no expense with hors d'oeuvere's, a meal, and a bar.

After the social hour, the Master of Ceremonies, Art Anselmo, a Deputy State Attorney General, and himself a former District Court Judge, got on the mike and asked the guests to take their seats at tables which already had name tags in front of each plate. Dinner was served.

After dinner and the tables cleared by waitresses, Anselmo started the wine tasting program. He was hilarious. with the introduction of each vintage of wine, as the waitresses passed out several bottles to each table, he came up with jokes that would put Jerry Lewis or Bob Hope to shame.

As I learned quickly, at a wine tasting party, in order to cleanse your pallet for the next wine to be sampled, you need to rinse your mouth with water, and there were several pitchers at each table, then expel, spit, that rinse water into an empty pitcher. Soon the empty pitchers would resemble containers of wine.

When the hour come to around ten P.M., Carol and I excused ourselves saying that we had to get home to the kids.

The following Monday morning at about eleven thirty, I got a call in the Narco office. It was Harvey.

"Eli, can you come up to my place, I've been robbed?"

"What do you mean, Harv, your shop, were they armed?"

"Not my shop, my apartment, and no, I didn't see who did it. It was overnight in the party room and they got all the valuable silverware and crystal goblets that I left in there after the party on Saturday night."

Not wanting to try to have him understand the difference between robbery and theft or burglary, it would take too long, I went on to the next question. "How did they get in, I thought when you use the party room that you had the only key to the adjacent room so that you could move all your stuff in there until you came in the next day to clean up?" I asked.

"I was so tired, I thought I'd leave everything in the main room of the two banquet rooms and that nobody would bother with my stuff. But, I forgot that all tenants have a key to the main door leading into the banquet room."

"What's missing, Harv?"

"A couple cases of unopened wine. My mothers cut glass, crystal goblets, that she brought to this country when she migrated from Russia before the communist revolution. That crystal had been in our family for over four generations. My mother will have a heart attack if I don't get them back. They're priceless. And Don Odden's silverware, in addition to my own. I had borrowed Odden's forks, knives and spoons, and it's very valuable silverware. I knew that with fifty some guests I would need to borrow some of that stuff. Odden will shit." He moaned. "Can you come?"

"Harv, did you try any of the guys in the Detective Bureau, maybe they could look into it. I and my guys have an ongoing investigation with some feds that we can't break away from right now, and besides, this would be out of our bailiwick."

"I tried the Detective Bureau and they are all busy on two rapes and a robbery that happened last night. What kind of department have you got when I can't even get someone to come up here?" He demanded.

"Don't get all wound up now, Harv, I'll get the desk officer to send up the district patrol squad and they can help." I tried.

"I don't want any uniform guys to come up here since I already know who did it." He exclaimed.

Surprised, I said, "Who did it, and how do you know?"

"The custodian, all night through the whole party, he sat across the way by the pool, at a table just watching," he shouted, "Didn't you notice him through the big glass window that overlooks the pool from the party room? It had to be him!"

We had been seated across the room from the window and didn't see the custodian.

"Uh huh, the butler, the maid, or the janitor. You always say that you'd be a good man in the FBI, this takes the cake. We never want to rule anyone out, but you may have been watching too much 'Murder She Wrote' on TV. Why don't I see if I can get Dan Price to break away from whatever he's doing and come up there?" I suggested.

"Danny's the best, but can he do it? The Lieutenant in the Detective Bureau said all his guys were busy, that that I should ask the custodian to keep the room locked 'till he can get someone up here. Can you let me know?" he asked.

I'll get back to you in a few minutes." I told him.

It turned out that Dan Price, his partner, and several other detective teams were busier'n hell on the rapes of the night before, so I called Harvey back and told him to make sure that the room is kept secure and, if no detectives were to be free the next day, Tuesday, I would grab someone from my Narco Unit and check out his loss by theft.

"Talk with that custodian first, I know it's him. I just talked with Don Odden and is he ever pissed." Judge Odden, who grew up with Harvey in the tough Central Hillside neighborhood, was now a victim of a crime.

"And, you know what else they took?"

"I couldn't even begin to guess."

"All those pitchers which were on the tables that people spit the rinse water in before sampling a different wine. I hope the thieving bastards drank all that!" He shouted.

We continued our conversation and I assured him that I would look into it the next day if the regular detectives were busy.

On Tuesday, after learning that it would be futile to wait for a detective squad to be clear, I called Harvey, told him I was coming up to his apartment, but he said that he had a couple big orders to fill out, he owned an electrical motors supply company, and would need to be in his office. However, he told me where we could find the custodian's office in the building.

I took Rod Radich, a member of the Narco Unit, with me and it didn't take us long to find the custodian.

After identifying ourselves and telling him what we were up to, he said, "I told that darn Harvey to move all his valuables into the back room if he wasn't going to clean up that night. He has the only key to that room and it's the way we make sure that our tenants don't lose anything after a party. After they get their stuff out of that secure room, they return the key to me.

But, for the main banquet room, all tenants have a key. It's one of the perks of living here."

I asked, "Would you have any idea of who could have pulled this?" Rod added, "It almost has to be one of your tenants."

"I don't disagree, but I wouldn't have the faintest." He replied.

With nothing to go on, I asked if he would show us the tenants list. "Sure, we have forty two units and many are cases of shared occupancy. I've got names of all occupants."

Looking over the list, two names hit me almost as if they were in bold black print. I said nothing about it and asked, "Would it be ok if we knocked on a few doors to see if anyone saw or noticed anybody late Saturday night hauling things out of the party room?"

"Be my guest, but a lot of our tenants are at work. Good Luck."

We walked down the hall on the first floor and when the custodian wasn't in sight at the other end, I quickly led Radich up a flight of stairs to the second floor.

When we reached the landing on Floor Two, I stopped and explained to Rod that I recognized two names in room 204, a couple young good time guys from West Duluth who I wouldn't put it past them, coming home late from a night out on the town, to check on remains from a party. And, who knows what they might think or do, seeing all that wine and valuables. "We got nothing now so we might as well play it by ear." Rod Agreed.

We went to Room 204. I knocked.

A voice came through the door and I knew it wasn't Ken's, as I had known him since he was in diapers. "Who is it?" The voice asked.

"Jimmy?" I put it in the form of a question.

"Yeah." He said. But, as he opened the door and, seeing us, tried to slam it shut. My shoe was in the way.

Now was not the time to be diplomatic or timid. "You guys ripped off all the wine, silverware and crystal from Harvey Solon in the party room Saturday night, and we need to get it back! Where's Ken?"

"He's working, we didn't know that was from Harvey Solon, but we can give it back except for some of the wine. We had a party in our apartment on Sunday night and a lot of the wine went."

"Yeah, where's all the silverware and the rest of the wine? And we better get it all!"

"Some of the unopened wine bottles are there in these cardboard boxes, pointing to boxes in a corner of the living room, but some of the pitchers are in the fridge."

"The fridge, what pitchers?" I started to grin as I asked.

"The pitchers that were on each table top. We wanted to use them up before we opened any bottles." He matter of factly said.

I asked again about the silverware and he led us to the automatic dishwasher where we recovered Judge Odden's complete setting of sixteen spoons, forks and knives.

"What about the crystal wine goblets?" I demanded.

"Didn't see any, someone else must have gone in the party room too."

"Don't bullshit us, I have a half notion to let Harvey know it was you guys and maybe he can turn one of the wrestlers loose on you." I kidded.

"I swear I didn't see any crystal."

Our entry to the apartment was dubious at best. No probable cause, no warrant to search, just a small degree of street smarts that led us to believe that recovery of the stolen items was better than nothing. Jimmy and Ken's apartment would not have qualified for a search based on a skimpy hunch, and any judge would have chased us out of their office if we brought a search warrant application to them for the apartment. So, a bluff was required, and bluff we did.

"OK, the wine in the fridge, let's look in there." I said.

Four pitchers of red liquid were sitting on two shelves within the refrigerator. I calmly took two, handed them to Rod, took the other two and walked to the kitchen sink and spilled the rinse water/wine combination.

"What are you doing?" Asked an excited Jim.

"Dumping spit." I said, and went on to explain, also reminding him that his friends will really appreciate hearing about how they were served this superb wine.

The thought of it made Jim gag.

I advised him that we were going to confer with our boss, Inspector Russ Barber, to determine if a warrant was to be requested for them for theft. BS again.

Jim found a couple large cardboard boxes and we loaded them up and headed for Harvey's shop, a bit proud that we had recovered the items we were carrying.

When we got to his office and he saw the returned property, he shouted, "You guys are the best. Don Odden just called and asked if there were any leads. I'm going to call him back now, but first, did they break or damage any of my mother's crystal wine goblets?"

"That's the problem, Harv, they didn't have them, and they say they didn't see any." I sadly reported.

He looked almost in tears, "Hell, can't Duluth's finest do anything? My mother is pretty old. Shit, this will kill her."

We knew his mother to be about eighty five and in frail condition.

I told him that our entry into the apartment was shaky, thus we couldn't expect any follow up and couldn't give him the names as well. I did have second thoughts on Jim's denial about the goblets, so I told Harvey we would go back and talk with our suspects again.

Knocking at Room 204 on our return, Jim answered without question and we walked in.

"Are you guys going to arrest me?" He asked.

"Only if we don't get the crystal wine goblets back for Harvey. If his mother dies of a heart attack I wouldn't want to be in your shoes. The safest place for you would be in jail, I lied.

"Why don't I call Ken at his work place? Maybe he knows." Offered Jim.

"Ken, this is Jim, Miletich is here again and wants to talk with you." "Here." He turned the phone over to me.

"Ken, I think I'm going to let your folks know what in hell you've been up to. What kind of jerks do you take us for? I know you've got those crystal goblets stashed and I want to know right now! You've got exactly five seconds to cough up or I'm talking to your folks and then to a prosecutor, finally I will let Solon know who ripped him off. It's up to you"

"In the closet, under a bunch of dirty laundry." He said. "I was going to give them to my fiancee as a wedding present, they're already gift wrapped."

After locating the goblets in the closet, beautifully wrapped in a box with a ribbon and bow, I got back on the phone, Ken was waiting. "Ken, it's a good thing our families have been close since before I was born. Also, without the approval of Harvey, since he is the complainant, your ass would be going to jail right now. The next time you won't be so lucky!" I lied again.

"Now, let me tell you another thing that should make you feel good." I then went on to tell him about the pitchers of wine rinse he served his guests the night after the theft. I could audibly hear him gagging over the phone.

Back to Harvey's office we went.

"Look what we've got, Harv." I quietly said as I set the box containing the gift wrapped goblets on his desk.

238

"Damn, I never thought I'd see this again." He said as he unwrapped the box. "Like I said, you guys are the best!" He was now shouting. "How in hell did you do it?"

"Can't tell you Harv, but the important thing is you got your stuff as well as your mothers crystal and Judge Odden's silverware. If we had been strictly conventional, we'd never have been able to do it because we had no real suspects and just acted on a hunch."

"What about Don Odden? He wants to know who these guys are and why you don't arrest them."

I said "Call the judge right now and I'll explain why we can't make an arrest. He'd be the first person to throw a situation like this out of court for lack of probable cause."

Harvey got the judge on first try.

"Hi judge, Eli here."

"What in hell is going on that you can't arrest those assholes, Eli?" He asked.

"Judge, we had no suspects and only saw the names of these guys on the tenant list, and because I knew them, we made a stab in the dark and it paid off, we recovered everything. But as you will agree, we couldn't have got a thing back if we weren't a bit unorthodox in the way we handled it."

"Don't get me wrong," he said, "I think that under the circumstances you did great, but it frustrates me that we can't get some court action on these guys. You can at least tell me their names, can't you?"

"Judge, you're an honorable man, but I can just see these guys coming before you on some unrelated offense and you throwing the book at them because you're still pissed off."

I laughed.

"You know me better than that, come on."

"No way, judge."

"Well, some day I'll get you to tell me."

"Don't hold your breath your honor." I laughed.

Harvey, the unofficial coordinator of the lunch bunch at places like the Chinese Lantern, the Zelda or the Whaleback Room, would usually make the initial call to one person and set off the chain of phone calls that got the group together. It was always a roaring time with nearby tables often joining in on the story or joke telling.

Often times at these lunches, until Judge Odden's passing just a few years ago, he would lean over in my direction, grinning, and say in a loud whisper, "Are you ready to tell me who those assholes were that ripped off my silverware?"

Chapter Seventeen

## October 4

That morning there was electricity in the air, as the several officers getting ready to follow up on the reports of the Hall and Ecklund interview with Rosendin were listening to some instructions from Inspector Fred Sowl, during a briefing with Sergeant Alexander.

"Because we now have a pretty definite suspect," explained Sowl, "and we know that he met our witness in Colorado where he, the suspect, was in control of a vehicle, the Toyota Wagon believed to be owned by the victim, which victim resided in Colorado, we can formally ask the FBI to assist in the search for the Toyota and the suspect. He obviously crossed state lines to get here from Colorado, and it's our belief that she was likely dead and in the back of the Wagon when he left Colorado.

"If he is still in possession of that vehicle he probably is crossing more state lines with it."

242

"We've talked to Bob Harvey and they are already setting up their network to try and track him down. Let's continue with the calm deliberate work that you all are displaying and we'll get this guy"

"Chief, did you want to say something at this time before Sergeant Alexander goes on with the assignments for today?"

"Thanks, Fred. I just want to echo what Fred said about the good work thus far, but I do want to caution you that we want to choose very carefully anything we say for public consumption, in other words, statements to the press, things that may tip the guy off that we have him as a suspect or that we have a witness, that is if he's still in the area, which I doubt."

"Also, we don't want anything to happen to the witness. With that in mind, I've told Alexander that we are not to share his identity with anyone, not even the County Attorney's office, or should I rephrase that and say, especially not the County Attorney's office, at least not until we have the suspect in custody or we go for an arrest warrant. They shouldn't be able to screw it up then."

Eli J. Miletich

*How do you know when an attorney is lying?*

I digress here, because I have some strong feelings about some of the people who have worked in the St. Louis County Attorneys' office over the years of my career.

Geographically, St. Louis county is the largest county in Minnesota. In fact, "It is the largest county east of the Mississippi River in the United States," as the now retired Sheriff, Gregg Sertich, used to say when making appeals to his county board of commissioners and the state legislature for funds for his department.

The man was usually right on the button in his appeals. However, when you're dealing with legislators and commissioners in the state of Minnesota who are more concerned with the rights of bad guys and allegedly endangered plants and dumb animals than the rights of innocent citizens, and the unborn, it makes for a tough row to hoe for a guy who is responsible for rural, and some smaller communities' law enforcement, in a county larger than such states as Rhode Island, Delaware, Maryland, Vermont, New Hampshire and Connecticut. Such is the magnitude of the county, and it is most noticeable in an undermanned Sheriff's Department.

When discussing my reservations about the office of County Attorney, I also reflect on some great prosecutors over the years who kept their nose to the grindstone, did their research and homework. They worked diligently with the police to advise and instruct as to the need for thorough and complete investigations and reports in order to comply with statutory and judicial requirements. They also kept their personal lives unsullied. Jerry Arnold, John DeSanto, Mark Rubin, Bill Summerness and Doug Merritt come to mind, among a few others.

Then there were the assistant county attorneys, prosecutors, who read a case file only minutes prior to a court appearance by a defendant, and some guys who showed up for a court case at nine thirty in the morning, go to a local pub during the noon recess, drink their lunch out of a stein and return to court. Plea bargains were plentiful with shrewd defense attorneys taking every opportunity to gain an advantage.

One prosecutor, Velik Kurac, a big man physically, little muscle and mostly flab, a weasel in office and a mink in his private life, was such a person. His love of alcohol was said to be his excuse.

To give a more succinct view of my involvement with such prosecutors, I can recall several incidents.

By the end of the 60's, the drug problem had finally come full force into the Northland. We've always been among the last to be touched by fads be it the hula hoop, rock and roll, clothes, you name it. Likewise, when we started to hear and read of reports of the so called new drug culture, we chuckled and made such comments as "it will never reach here."

Little did we know. But of course drugs are a curse, not a fad!

Throughout that decade, investigations and reports dealt more and more with drug related offenses. Street officers, as well as investigators, handling those cases were doing a commendable job with the little bit of background and training as had been provided by the department. Like the Sheriff's Department outside the city, budgets controlled by the politicians, in this case the City Council, did not include narcotics training.

Notwithstanding the budgetary shortcomings, the Police Department tried to keep up with what was happening. They, the department administration, saw that there was a lack of coordination and cohesion in compiling information and coping with what was fast becoming a whole new area of criminal activity. A need for intelligence gathering and undercover work to sniff out suspects and develop cases by which to take them, the suspects, to court was quite apparent.

My predecessor, Police Chief Milo Tasky, an excellent administrator and a nice guy, had put together a committee of his staff to study the problem and make recommendations. Chaired by the most knowledgeable and ablest police officer it has ever been my privilege to know and work with, but especially to learn from, Detective Bureau boss, Inspector Russ Barber, the committees recommendation was to form a separate, special unit, a Narcotics Squad.

That units' function would be to receive all reports involving drugs and narcotics, follow up on those cases which needed

247

*Eli J. Miletich*

follow up, set up an intelligence program on suspects and their hang outs and activities. It was to be responsible for dissemination of all such pertinent information to department personnel so that a unified effort could be put forth in fighting this growing problem.

The Narcotics Unit was to be attached to the Detective Bureau with a degree of autonomy, responding only to the Inspector and, of course, the Chief of Police. Flexible hours and shifts, within reason, were also established. The rationale for that was that drug dealers do not work shifts.

I was working as a Sergeant/Detective Investigator one day in December 1969, when Inspector Barber called me into his office for a meeting.

After giving me a rundown on what had been recommended by the Chief's staff committee, he said that because I had been turning out a pretty good work product on most of my cases, including a couple drug incidents, one involving a barbiturate fatality following a huge drug party, they had decided to offer the leadership of the unit to me. I accepted without hesitation in as much as my objective was to learn as much about all facets

248

of police work as I could. I was ambitious and honest ambition is a noble characteristic in my estimation.

The Narco Unit went into action in February staffed by two police officers and myself.

We immediately enlisted the staff of the Record Bureau to cull and isolate reports related to drugs and narcotics, whether they referred to suspected dealers or users, or persons who had information about the aforesaid.

Initially we had no secretary assigned to the unit, so the Chief's secretary, a brilliant organizer, Ann Milich, used her coffee breaks to start a file system for reports, as well as a confidential catalog of informants. Informants are a vital cog in the wheel of law enforcement and they come from all walks of life. They are people who offer information on drug activity for a variety of reasons such as the dislike and fear of what drugs do to people. Revenge, envy, as well as the financial incentive of receiving rewards for aiding police, are just several of the motives. Thus confidentiality is a priority in a cops mind.

Quite often Ann even stayed past her shift to help set us up properly. Her system prevails to this day.

*Eli J. Miletich*

In its' entire history, even the oldest veterans would agree, the police department had not executed more than fifteen or twenty search warrants, nor did they really have any experience in preparing reports requesting approval from the courts for such documents. They simply went to the home of a suspect, knocked on a door and if there was no response from within, kicked it open and went about with their search, and arrest, if they felt they had cause to make one.

Court decisions of the sixties changed all that, and properly so.

In the first year of the Narco Units existence sixty some search warrants were applied for before the courts with most resulting in evidence which justified either an arrest on the spot or later by warrant. These warrants came about by police officers complying with the dictates of statutes and court decisions, not by whim or fancy of the moment. That number would climb dramatically over the ensuing years.

It was a sharp, dedicated young prosecutor, Jerry Arnold, who not only carried the load on the drug cases for the County Attorneys office, but he also served as an educator for the staff of the police department, bringing us out of the ignorance of bygone years when all one had to do to be a cop was to be huge, follow all orders and do whatever it took to get the job done.

However, the problem with the police/prosecutor relationship is that the cop doesn't get to choose who he wants to work with from the prosecutors office. Some of my most exasperating days as a cop were dueling with lazy, indifferent, inept, drunken or suspected corrupt members of the County Attorney's staff.

————————————

In the mid 1970's there was almost a revolving door to the County Attorney's office with respect to staff attorneys. Some lawyers, fresh out of law school, saw a prosecutor position as an opportunity to learn criminal law without the overhead expense of opening a private practice. They worked in the office a couple years, gained some experience as well as contacts and then set off on their own.

Some, apparently lacking any confidence in their ability, found the bimonthly check from the County Treasurer a security blanket, never venturing into the sometimes wild and woolly field of private law where they may have to compete with others, perhaps equally inept. Several still are on the St. Louis County Attorney's staff.

Incompetents like a Gerry Snell who came to town, much heralded as a prosecutorial genius from Minneapolis, flopped after several unsuccessful months and some personal problems, disappeared from the scene and was never to be heard from again in the area.

Others, the Mike Dean's and Verne Swanum's continue to feed at the public trough and show very little in the way of productivity.

I'll talk a bit about two categories on my list from above, the drinkers and suspected corrupt.

One of my responsibilities, in addition to overseeing the activities of the Unit, which had grown to six members by the mid 70's, was to coordinate drug investigative activities with other agencies on the federal, state and regional level. Such was the situation one August when, as a result of a series of undercover buys of small quantities of hashish, marijuana and

LSD, enough probable cause was established to receive approval for a search warrant of a premises in the West End. The suspect had made sales to a state agent at that particular residence.

Now, one could say, "Why didn't they go in with a search warrant right after the first buy of illegal drugs?" The answer is security and confidentiality. The State of Minnesota Crime Bureau agent who was the undercover man in this operation would have been compromised, burned, and rendered useless for undercover work in this area. Equally important, the informant who had introduced the agent to the dealer would also have been exposed making it highly likely that the informant would be in danger. Thus the cleanest way is to try to make a series of buys, with one agent introducing a second agent who in turn makes introduction of a third. By that time, who brought whom becomes a bit cloudy. Besides, in this instance the dealer was a low man on the ladder and we wanted to get the man who delivered the stuff, and that requires patience.

*Eli J. Miletich*

With an affidavit prepared detailing the investigative efforts utilized by our officers as well as state agents, we went to the residence of Luther Eckman, Judge of District Court. It was early evening and the judge had just sat down to supper, but he allowed us to interrupt.

After a review of the probable cause outlined in the Affidavit and Application for Search Warrant, the judge approved our request and signed off in the appropriate box which authorized us to serve the warrant without first announcing our presence, i.e., a 'no knock search warrant.'

In other words, we would not be required to shout "police", which in drug searches would be tantamount to shouting to the suspect to open the toilet lid and start flushing!

It was a very successful search. In addition to the dealer we apprehended his supplier who had pockets of an old army field jacket loaded with hundreds of sugar cubes laced with LSD, and who was also carrying a satchel quarter filled with small Hershey type slabs of hashish. We had hit them at the right time, delivery time.

We also realized a bonus with the arrest of seven other persons who had just made some buys and who were, at the time of our unexpected arrival, pulling on some lit marijuana cigarettes. Each of them was charged with Possession of Controlled Substances, felonies as well as misdemeanors, according to the drugs found in their pockets during the time of their respective individual searches. Naturally, the weed they were sucking on became part of the floor litter when we came crashing in, so they could not be charged for those items.

Among those charged for possession were three females and four males, this apart from the dealer and supplier who were charged with Sale of Controlled Substances and Delivery of Controlled Substances, both felonies.

Most of the seven customers received stiff probationary sentences. That's tongue in cheek, folks. Only one received time and that was at the Northeast Regional Correctional Center, formerly the St. Louis County Work Farm, which we had sometime before began calling "Holiday Inn North."

One of the females, a blonde with a Hollywood, Donna Summers, figure, was quite concerned about her opportunity for future employment with a conviction for a drug offense as we were to find out some months later. And, we did find out. Several of our informants were active people.

Informant number 114 soon brought us news that this blonde was working on having her record expunged and that she was doing this by way of keeping company, occasionally with one of the attorneys from the County Attorneys office, matter of fact, Velik Kurac, the guy who originally prosecuted the case she was involved in. "I think he's scoring with her," said the informant.

There was a downtown bar, Mr. Pete's, where many of the people in the legal profession liked to unwind at the end of the day. We knew that Velik Kurac was one who frequented the place on a regular basis. It didn't take long to corroborate the info from our informant about Kurac and the blonde.

We advised our superiors and were properly admonished not to spend time surveilling the private life of the gentleman in question, but that we should log the information in our memory bank and on confidential reports as, after all, as a prosecutor he was a public official fraternizing with an individual whom he had prosecuted.

Kurac's stock and credibility went down to zero when, several months later, the blondes record was indeed expunged. Of course, another staff assistant county attorney was the one submitting the approval papers to the court. That's not the end of this tale, however.

———————————————

Approximately fifteen months later we were working with federal agents Bud King, John Dziak, and Milton Woo of the U.S. Customs Bureau Investigative Unit, and were developing a number of good leads on suspects who were potential federal violators hence, the feds interest.

Early in October of that year, I received a phone call from one of the informants who had been making some introductions to dealers for us. He wanted to meet with us in a hurry as he had some hot news about a former Duluth guy who had some big connections and would sell the informant up to five hundred pounds of marijuana. He couldn't explain because people were watching him talk on a pay phone and he didn't want to be

Eli J. Miletich

overheard. I told him that Denny Lepak and I would meet him by the Blatnik High Bridge.

The Blatnik High Bridge is named after the long time, now deceased, congressman John Blatnik who did so much for his district as a legislator. He was a key sponsor of the bill which approved construction of the St. Lawrence Seaway as well as the Interstate Highway System. A hero of World War II, he had served with the OSS, the predecessor to the CIA, and had parachuted behind enemy Nazi lines to serve as liaison with guerrilla forces operating in Yugoslavia.

The bridge is one of two high suspension bridges which span the St. Louis River at it's widest parts between Duluth and Superior, Wisconsin with the surface of each at about one hundred twenty feet above the water. By meeting under the approach on the Duluth side, we would be assured of some privacy and for the informant, confidentiality.

As we pulled up abreast of the informants beat up old brown Chrysler, I said, "What have you got?"

"I've got a contact who can arrange delivery of five hundred pounds of grass if I can come up with the cash. You know me

258

though, I've quit using any of that stuff, so I thought maybe you'd be interested. And, get this, that's only half the story. The rest will blow your mind!" said the informant, who I will call Harry Speekup.

"Come, get in the back of our car," said Lepak. And while Speekup was moving between cars, Denny flipped the 'on' button to our portable tape recorder. It's not good practice to be taking notes in front of an informant, it makes them get up tight.

"Okay, let's hear what this is all about," I said.

"Do you guys know a former Duluth doper named Jeremiah Wanger? He was supposed to be heavy into all kinds of dope a couple years ago until the feds got him in Washington state. He served time there for dealing heroin, but he's out now and is in Texas. He goes by the name of Jerry W."

"Yeah, we've heard of him, but not lately," Denny answered. Of course, Denny was telling a bit of a white lie. You don't feed informants information on what you know or don't know. They're the ones who are supposed to furnish you with the info. We were quite familiar with Jerry W., having been kept up to date on his activities in the Seattle/Tacoma area by the feds.

matter of fact, it was one of John Dziak's Customs buddies, when John was working as an agent in Washington, who had made several buys from Jerry W. and then busted him and his supplier. "Go On." said Denny.

"Well, he was in town two days ago and we met at a mutual friends place and smoked some pot together——" "I thought you said that you quit that shit," I cut him off.

"I have, but I have a relapse once in a while," he replied with a grin on his face.

"You know that if we ever find you dirty, your ass has had it," said Lepak.

"I know."

"What's the rest?" I pursued.

"Anyway, we got to talking and he tells me that he has a connect in El Paso who has a heavy source in Mexico who can deliver up to five hundred pounds of grass at a time to a willing and able buyer. Able, meaning having the cash up front.

So I tell him that I'd be interested, but that I don't have that kind of cash, though I might be able to get a friend or two to go in with me. That's when I thought of you guys.

He went back to El Paso yesterday, but I have his phone number and he told me the times he can be reached, he stays by the phone during those hours, and his customers as well as the people he buys from know the right hours.

I figure you guys will want to do something about this information," he finished

"I figure you're giving us a line of BS because you can use some spare cash," I said, "I don't think you know Jerry W., that you probably just picked up his name on the street, heard a bit about him, and now you want to get a few bucks from us with this cock and bull story." I tested him some more.

"No, it's the absolute truth. Look, you know I've only been living in Duluth for the past eight months, but I've turned some pretty decent cases for your undercover guy and I haven't crossed you up, have I?

I also know that Jerry W.'s sister has been keeping company with one of the guys from the County Attorney's office, and he helped get her record cleared of a minor possession conviction. He told me that. Another thing. He gave me the name of the guy from Mexico who is the big supplier.

He's a general in the army by the name of Francisco Huerta. Have it checked out."

"We will," I answered, "But since you're the one he will deal with, you are going to have to be the one who serves as the middle man, if we can get the feds to get into this, that is.

You know, we're sixteen hundred or so miles from El Paso, and we don't know if the agencies down there have the time to get involved with such a small amount as this," I kidded him.

"That's no small amount by anyone's standards, and you know it!" he laughed. "Sure, I'll do the introduct, but I want my expenses covered."

We all knew and recognized that informants gave information for a variety of reasons, but most were the financial rewards that would be forthcoming if arrest and prosecution were successful.

"Look, we will have to go back to our office to make some phone calls to see what we can get going. We'd like you to go to your apartment and wait there for about the next two hours. It's going to take at least that long, then one of us will call you.

One last thing. Did he say how much notice he would need to take delivery of that kind of quantity?" I asked.

"At least forty eight hours."

"Good, talk to you later and, by the way, thanks," I said.

Back at our office I called the number of Bud King, Customs Bureau . He wasn't in, but his secretary, Big Red, responded with "Special Agent in Charge, Mr. King, is out of the office right now, may I have him return your call?"

"My, aren't we formal today," I teased her.

"Darn you, Eli, I didn't recognize your voice. Bud is out of the office, really, but I can reach him by radio if it is important. I can have him call you."

"It is important, and since you will be talking with him, ask him if he can stop in at the Duluth PD Narco office if he is close to the Civic Center."

A few minutes later King walked through our door.

"What's up, this better be good because I don't have time to be chasing wild geese for the Duluth PD hot shots."

"Hey Bud, when did we ever call on you if we didn't need the expertise of one of this country's most illustrious agents to

*Eli J. Miletich*

help us catch some bad guys?" said Gene Sisto. "You know we couldn't get things done around here unless we got help from you!" he added. This kind of bantering always went on between King and the guys in Narco.

When King was transferred from Denver to Duluth, he and his team, Milt Woo and John Dziak, were the only federal agents working on illegal drug activities in all of northern Minnesota, Wisconsin and Michigan's upper peninsula. The federal government had yet to realize that drug traffickers could, and would, find it handy to cross at the border with Canada.

The three Customs guys were experienced and street wise and they enjoyed a high level of rapport with city and county police narcotics cops in the area. They were always ready to give a hand, and vice versa. Oftentimes, they would sit on a dreary, boring surveillance of a suspect with us for hours during a cold winter night when you had to sit in a car with the engine shut off because you didn't want the exhaust smoke to give you away.

When we gave him the information about Jerry W. and the Mexican general and the potential buy of five hundred pounds of marijuana, King said, "I'll call our people in El Paso and see what they have to say. I'm not familiar with this General Huerta or whatever his name is, but if he is a suspect they will have his name. That's a problem, you know, a lot of their military people are involved in drug trafficking and neither their government or ours wants to do anything about it. We can only speculate on the reasons for that. Is it okay if I give them the name of your snitch?"

"Bud, you know we'd entrust you with our lives, but we don't know your counterparts in El Paso, in fact, you don't either, so I'd just as soon wait 'till we get something firmed up as far as a possible buy and bust, before we let them know who our guy is. If Jerry W. is working both sides of the street, he could be on a fishing expedition. We did hear a few days ago that he was out on the street again and that the Drug Enforcement Agency, DEA, had turned him and that he was setting up some undercover buys in Seattle. But, if this info from the informant today is true, he's definitely working both sides, and right under their noses!" I stressed.

"No problem," responded King, "But you got to realize that your snitch needs to set up the introduction of one of our undercover agents to the suspect if this thing materializes and, they are going to need his name for their confidential reports at that time."

"That's fine, but for now, we can vouch for his reliability as an informant on previous cases resulting in convictions, and we'll feel a lot better if they know nothing personal about him until it, the bust, comes down. If your guys in El Paso have someone to work undercover with the informant making the introduction, our only logistical concern will to get him from here to Texas."

"Are you going to tell me who your snitch is?" Do I know him?"

"Yeah, it's Speekup, Harry Speekup, he's done a few things on cases you've worked with us."

"I'd agree he's reliable," said King, "Isn't he the one who's father is a prominent attorney in Madison, Wisconsin? I thought he was going in for treatment."

"We've been talking to him to convince him to do just that, or go home and have his folks do something for him, but he says that his father won't have anything to do with him," said Sisto, "But he maintains that he is trying to get straight by himself. "don't know if that is going to work though."

"I'll get back to you as soon as I get through to El Paso." Said King, and he departed for his own office in the Federal Building, across the Civic Center from City Hall, where the PD is located.

About an hour later the phone rang and Sisto answered. "If your snitch can leave in the morning, or sooner," It was King, "We'll give him gas money and cash for other incidental expenses, motel, food. Our guys in El Paso have confirmed that they have seen Jerry W. in the area. Seems the DEA in Seattle didn't know that he had left for the Southwest. They hadn't had contact with him for a while.

Anyway, they confirm that the general, Huerta, is a heavy, and is big in the Mexican military, also seems protected by the politicians. Probably is a big contributor.

They say that this would be the closest they have ever been to getting the general and they are eager to follow up on it."

"So what do you need from us?" Sisto asked.

"We need to meet with the snitch, debrief him further, have him make an appointment for a buy for about three or four days from now. He can tell Jerry W. that he has a biker friend from Canada who is coming with him and will be fronting him the cash. Naturally, one of our agents from the Texas office will play the Canadian.

We want Harry, your snitch, to drive his old junker from here to there. It's Interstate 35 most of the way. Better than flying 'cause they will wonder where he got the money for a ticket, even if he went by bus or train. Also, when he's on the road, we'd want him to call you about every four hours to let you know his whereabouts. We want this for two reasons. First, so we can keep tabs on him. Second, we want him to pick up the agent who's going to be the Canadian after he goes through

Oklahoma City, but we don't want him to know that until he's close to that point. Then they'll travel the rest of the way together to El Paso.

Our agent will have only a small amount of flash money with him so that he won't be ripped off. His cover story is that when he sees the product, marijuana, he will have the money wired to El Paso by his partners from Thunder Bay," concluded King.

Sisto then called Harry Speekup and set up a meeting at King's office where a phone call was made and recorded. Because Jerry W. needed to make arrangements, he asked for a number to call back to and Harry, according to directions given to him in advance, gave Jerry W. the number to a 'cool phone' in King's office which was answered with a simple 'hello' or 'yeah'.

Jerry W. promised to call back inside an hour, and he did. Forty six minutes.

It was agreed that they meet at a certain motel in a little more than three days from the time of their conversation, at eight in the evening on the third day.

*Eli J. Miletich*

It would take some steady driving by the informant, with short rest periods, but he assured us he could do it.

After some more detailed but simple briefing by King, the informant was provided with some expense money and left for Texas.

On his way, during daylight hours, he called every three hours, in other words, every time he stopped to gas up. He'd sleep for several hours at roadside rest areas and be on the road.

Near the end of the second day he called from about thirty miles north of Oklahoma City and was given instructions on where to pick up his 'partner'. He would be waiting at a Burger King just off an exit from I-35, five miles south of Oklahoma City. All was going well thus far.

On the evening of the third day, King called to say that he had just received word that the informant and the 'Canadian' had arrived in El Paso, checked into another motel and were now under constant, but loose, surveillance by agents. The guys down there didn't want anything to foul this one up. The meet between all parties was only several hours off.

270

King also related that the undercover agent had shown his flash roll to the informant, but had cautioned him not to talk about money to the suspects when they meet, He, the agent, would do all the talking. A flash roll is a relatively small amount of money which is shown to a potential target to show good faith. In this case, the agent was carrying about five hundred dollars, with assurance that he could produce more when necessary.

The next morning Denny Lepak, Gene Sisto and I had arrived at work at about seven thirty intending to do some catch up on several reports which had been held in abeyance while we had been working on the El Paso thing.

At about eight thirty the phone on my desk rang. I picked it up, half anticipating a call from Bud King. Instead, it was Assistant County Attorney Velik Kurac who had been seen in the company of Jerry W.'s sister months earlier and, whom we believed helped to get her record expunged.

"Eeelii," he drawled out my name, "This is Velik Kurac,"— "Who," I cut him off, recognizing his voice, but my thoughts were already racing. "Velik Kurac," he replied, "I want to know something and don't bullshit me."

"What's that, Mr. Prosecutor?" I asked.

"Have you got an informant named Harry Speekup?"

"Come on, Kurac," I calmly replied, "The name doesn't ring a bell, but even if it did, and the person was an informant, you know that I wouldn't give you or anyone else an informants identification, you should know better than that. The minute we start bandying informants names about, someone gets hurt. We don't want that, do we?"

"Don't give me any of your cute shit, Miletich, I'm an Assistant County Attorney and I am asking you if you have an informant by the name of Harry Speekup?" Shouted Kurac.

"Look, Mr. Assistant County Attorney, I don't give informants to anyone, not even a judge, so go screw yourself! Why do you ask?" I firmly said, my blood pressure going higher with each word this asshole said.

Now came what would have been a shocker, if I didn't know better. "I have received information that this guy, Harry Speekup, pulled a gun on someone in a motel room in El

Paso,Texas, last night, further that he is an informant or yours," Kurac insisted.

Oh, Oh, I thought.

I laughed, "You gotta be kidding, El Paso is better than sixteen hundred miles from Duluth, a bit out of our jurisdiction, I'd say. Wouldn't you? And if this guy was an informant of mine, he sure as hell wouldn't be operating in El Paso. You say he pulled a gun on somebody down there, were the El Paso cops notified?"

Kurac persisted, "Can you check with the other guys in your office and see if they have this Speekup for an informant?"

"Gene, have you been working with an informant named Harry Speekup?" I shouted across the room to Sisto.

"Never heard of him," replied Gene.

"What about you, Denny?" I called out in the other direction to Lepak.

"Who the hell is that?" said Lepak, "Who's asking?

"Velik Kurac, he says that this guy, Speekup, was involved in some kind of gun incident in El Paso, Texas, last night and that he was an informant of mine."

Lepak laughed, "What in hell kind of name is Speekup? Sounds like something from an old Martin and Lewis movie comedy I saw when I was a kid."

"No, Kurac, nobody in this office knows the guy, what's this all about, and how did you get this information?"

"Like I said, I have a source who says this Harry guy pulled a gun on someone in El Paso last night, and that he is an informant of someone in your office." Again, he was shouting in a shrill voice.

"Calm down now, Kurac. I'd suggest that you, or your source, ought to report this to the El Paso police if this incident really happened, but I can't see why you're so excited about it. The guy is not a Duluth Narco informant." I said, chuckling, to let him believe that I couldn't care less about something that allegedly happened in far away Texas.

He hung up without even a goodbye.

I explained to Gene and Denny what the call from Kurac entailed, even though they could perceive from my end of the conversation the gist of it. We were in agreement that he, Kurac, had to have received a call from Jerry W.'s sister, the

Donna Summers look alike, with a story like that. Jerry W. was using his sisters contact in the County Attorney's office to try to find out if Harry Speekup was an informant. Talk about counterintelligence!

All through the phone conversation with Kurac I had been making notes on what was said and, when the short meeting with the two fellow officers was over, I immediately went into my boss's office to advise Russ Barber of what had transpired.

"We ought to get a warrant for him, the SOB, but if we do, your informant is burned. You had better document all this on a confidential worksheet, with both me and the Chief getting a copy. Maybe the guy will hang himself soon."

I then called Bud King, "How did things go last night? Any Problems?"

"So far, so good," he said, "They met, our undercover agent was introduced by the snitch. Jerry W. acted as the middle man doing the facilitating. But, the general was not there. Seems he was a bit leery about coming to meet someone he had not met before so he sent a substitute, an army Lieutenant.

Eli J. Miletich

The general's emissary wanted to see the 'Canadian's' green, so they made arrangements to show him today, after the money is wired to an El Paso bank from Thunder Bay, Ontario.

The plan is that the 'Canadian' will rent a safe deposit box to place the cash in after if is forwarded in the morning, then meet the Mexican at the bank to show him that the money is available. I think they want some time to check out your snitch and his 'Canadian' friend."

"They've just done that," I said.

"Huh?"

I explained the whole conversation with Velik Kurac to King and he was outraged, but quickly came to the same conclusion we had only minutes ago, in our office. It was a tough pill to swallow not doing anything about the prick, Kurac.

I was apparently convincing in my insistence with Kurac that I didn't know Speekup, because the Mexican met the 'Canadian' in the bank, looked at the thousands in the safe deposit box, was satisfied that the buyer was genuine and the transfer of the product, marijuana, for cash, was set up to take place at five P.M. that day in a large shopping center parking lot.

After a serious attempt to seek out any law enforcement surveillance, and satisfied that it wasn't a set up, the Mexican went through with the sale.

Five arrests were made. Three, including the Mexican army Lieutenant, were grabbed in El Paso. Jerry W. and the informant were arrested about two hundred miles north of El Paso, with the contraband, five hundred pounds of marijuana. The informant was released the next day for lack of evidence. He had performed beautifully according to the undercover agent.

The general's emissary, the Lieutenant, faced with spending a good part of the rest of his life in an American prison, not to see his family for years, gave a complete statement implicating the general and several other high ranking military officers and politicians. Indictments were issued for their arrest, but to this day the Mexican government has yet to turn them over to U.S. officials. Does anyone really think that will happen?"

Jerry W. and his American contact were charged with conspiracy to distribute controlled substances, convicted and sentenced to two to five years in a federal pen.

One day, years later, I heard someone asking my secretary, Dolores Pohjola, "Is Chief Miletich in?" And, recognizing the voice, when she buzzed me on the intercom, I said, "Send Mr. Wanger in."

When he walked in, I poured him a cup of coffee and we talked about old times. He was a bit surprised that I recognized his voice after over seven years. He was now a small businessman, having started a railroad tie salvage operation, buying old ties from several railroads in the area and selling them to landscapers and construction firms.

When I asked, he readily confirmed that he had called his sister and asked her to check with Velik Kurac to see if Harry Speekup was an informant. She had assured him the Kurac had called us and that we knew nothing of him.

Velik Kurac didn't last too much longer in the County Attorney's office, as he apparently became a political liability.

I will point out that when my appointment as Police Chief was sent to the City Council by the Mayor, and I was scheduled for confirmation hearings, one of the negative letter writers was that prestigious member of the Bar. Ah, but that's another story.

## Chapter Eighteen

## October 7

About one in the afternoon a police teletype arrived from the Indianapolis, Indiana Police Department. Roxanna Livingston-Voorsanger's car, the dark blue Toyota station wagon, had been spotted in that city. There was further information and the teletype requested an early phone call to the Indianapolis PD.

Alexander called, "Hi, this is Sergeant Pat Alexander of the Duluth, Minnesota Police Department. I'm responding to a teletype we received just minutes ago reference a suspect vehicle which had been seen in your city,"

"Just a moment, sir," said the female who answered. No Boulder smart ass type wisecracks here.

"Hello, this is Sergeant Hren, I was the one who sent you the message."

Alexander identified himself again and asked, "Can you fill me in on what you have?"

"Well, when we received that bulletin on your suspect driving a Toyota wagon with Colorado plates, we got it out to all units on the street and didn't come up with anything until early this morning. Seems that your guy arrived here on the 4th, shacked up with a female he met before in San Diego. He talked her into allowing him to park the wagon in her garage. He stayed two nights. She got up early today to get ready for work, she is a waitress, and he was gone. So was all her money that she had around the house and her credit cards. She called our department.

He gave her the name of Mike Vukovich, but she thinks that is phony. She says that in addition to her cash and credit cards, he also ripped out a page from her address book that had his phone number in San Diego on it. The Toyota wagon is gone also."

"Bob Harvey, resident FBI agent is in the office with us now, and he's been listening over the speaker phone. He's indicated that your local FBI office will be delivering a drawing of the suspect to you. You will have it in twenty minutes. Can you show it to that woman and give us a call if it's a match?" asked Alexander. "And, thanks very much for your help."

At 3:15, Alexander got a call from Sergeant Hren. "We just returned from that woman's house. She took one look at the drawing and said, 'that's him.' She also gave us a photograph of him that had been taken earlier this year when they had met in San Diego. Man, your artist is to be commended for a super job, the drawing is a near perfect likeness!"

Alexander had a wild thought, "Sergeant, do you think it would be a problem to contact that woman again and have her check her address book to see if an imprint may be on the next page following the page he ripped out? It's a long shot and doesn't come from any extensive police training, just from watching old movies as a kid. You know, you always look under the sheet for an imprint."

"We'll try, and it might be worth a shot," said Hren, adding, "I'll get back to you as soon as we return."

At 3:45 P.M., Hren called back. "You will never believe this. There was no imprint on the next page, but when we were talking to her, she remembered that she also had his name on another page. She turned to it and there it was, with a San Diego address and phone number.

We had the phone company do a quick check on the number and it is listed to a Sam and Mary Smith. Maybe you can have your FBI man contact his counterparts in San Diego to check this out further."

"Again, we can't thank you enough for all the help you have been," said a grateful Pat Alexander as he placed the phone back on the cradle.

Cooperation!

## Chapter Nineteen

Cooperation is vital in law enforcement, but sometimes dumb luck, or a fluke, combined with cooperation can do wonders also.

One cold January night my wife, Carol, and our nine year old son Dana, came down with a virus that shot their temperature to 102.4 degrees. Accompanied by a sore throat, ear ache and chills, they were sapped of strength. They could hardly move.

I called Dr. Sam Litman, our pediatrician, the guy who had nurtured and cared for six of the nine kids of Ilija and Italika Miletich. "I'm not going to order a prescription for them until I have a look at what it is that is bothering them," he barked.

Dr. Sam came to our house on the night of the 17th, checked them over, gave them each a separate antibiotic and wrote out a prescription, then gave us, Carol and me, hell for not calling him sooner. He was a gruff but gentle and caring person.

I knew that the prescription couldn't be filled at that late hour, it was after ten p.m., and all the pharmacies in town would be closed. Dr. Sam had some of the same pills, physicians samples, in his satchel, so he gave us enough for the first half of the next day, and he sternly told me not to forget to pick up the rest in the morning.

Like I said, Dr. Sam was a gruff, tough guy with a big heart. Possibly the last of Duluth's doctors to make house calls. He often told me of how, as one of several boys in a poor Russian immigrant family prior to World War I, he sold newspapers on a downtown street corner to save money for a college education. And, being of the Jewish faith didn't make it any easier when applying for admission to a WASP medical school, but he persevered.

Here was a guy who had hard knocks but learned to cope with adversity and became a huge success, never forgetting his origins.

When I was a student at Denfeld High in the western, working class, neighborhood of Duluth, I was active in three sports, football, hockey and baseball. Dr. Sam lived about four blocks away from Public Schools Stadium and was a fixture at the end of one of the benches, didn't matter which one, tending to any injured player, free of charge. He had been doing this for over thirty years, that is, when not at a hospital or on a house call. I'm sure there is a special place in heaven where he is resting as one of God's favorites.

The next day, January 18th, I took advantage of a quiet morning to catch up on some paperwork while the guys from the Narco Unit were having coffee with some state undercover agents.

Just a bit after noon, when Denny Lepak and Rod Radich came in, I asked which one wanted to go for a ride with me while I picked up the prescription at Schraeder's Drugs. They knew that Carol and Dana, who was then nine years old, were pretty sick.

"I'll go with you, if that's an order, boss," joked Radich.

"Good, let's go now, I've got a meeting with the Chief this afternoon, and I want to get that medicine before I get tied up on something."

We got into our car in the police garage and backed out onto the turnaround ramp when a call belched out on the radio:

*"All units. There is a hold up alarm at the North Shore Bank of Commerce branch bank in Lakeside. What squads are responding beside Squad 65?"*

Squad 65 is the district patrol unit in that neighborhood, and the dispatcher had presumed in advance that they would break off anything they might be involved in.

Squads from adjoining districts, 63 and 46 also indicated they were heading out to the scene, Detective Squads 43 and 45 were going too. The local FBI office was going to be notified as well.

Police Radio followed quickly with information on the suspects:

*"Subjects are believed to be two young white males, both wearing ski masks pulled over their faces, and army field jackets. One of the subjects field jacket had a tear on the lower rear left side. Both subjects were carrying and brandishing revolvers. Subject with the tear in his field jacket was carrying a long barrel, target type, revolver.*

287

*Eli J. Miletich*

*Both subjects were seen getting into a blue Ford Pickup, late model.*

*Subjects are armed and must be considered dangerous."*

The bank was in the Lakeside district of the city, about five miles east of our location, and with other units responding directly to the scene, or to the periphery of the scene, we decided that we would go to one of the thoroughfares which leads west from Lakeside. Glenwood Street was chosen, rather than rush to see a bunch of police vehicles clustered around a crime scene with officers trying to look busy, or intelligent, especially when there are suspects to be found.

Several other units had also notified radio that they were checking possible get away routes.

We arrived at our destination, Jean Duluth Road and Glenwood Street, found a good cover and sat there for the next fifteen minutes, looking for the suspect Ford Pickup. Police Radio barked again:

*"Attention all units. Additional information on the bank robbery suspects. The blue Ford pickup was found parked about four blocks away from the bank in the Lakeside*

288

*neighborhood. A house by house by officers was made and they found a housewife who happened to be looking out the window of her home at a yellow Volkswagen, Beetle, idling in front of her home.*

*A young woman described as having dark hair, wearing a head scarf, was sitting behind the wheel. Suddenly the Ford Pickup drove up and parked behind the VW. Two young men jumped out, ran and got into the VW which then drove off in a westerly direction. All units are to check their districts for the yellow VW Beetle."*

"Damn," Radich said, "That yellow VW could have been driving circles around us and we're sitting here looking for that blue Ford pickup. They could be forty miles down I-35 towards the Cities by now."

"For sure, looks like a dead issue, let's go on our original mission, we may see that yellow VW near Schraeder's Pharmacy," I half joked.

We left our observation parking space and drove to Schraeder's which was in a small business district in the hillside area a few blocks up the hill from downtown. I got the prescriptions for Carol and Dana.

As I got back behind the wheel, I said, "I bet if we went to Piedmont Heights we'd probably see that yellow VW." That is my neighborhood, and it was kind of a police joke that when you wanted to get some P.B. done, (that's Personal Business), you said in all seriousness, that you were going to look for a suspect or suspicious activities in the area of your destination. Schraeder's is on 4th Street and 5th Avenue East, and my home is on 26th Street at 25th Avenue West. That's about five and one half miles distance in a northwesterly direction.

Piedmont Heights is a neighborhood atop one of the steep hills which make up most of the central to eastern parts of Duluth. Of the many roads which lead there, 5th Street, running east-west along the middle of the hillside until it hits the Skyline Drive at approximately 15th Avenue West, was the shortest and most direct route.

Thus, we made a right turn for one block, a left turn on 5th, and west we went.

But, as fate would have it, my medicine run was interrupted again.

While heading west on 5th, and nearing the 1200 block, I noticed the car at about the same instance that Rod Radich had. It was parked, it was yellow, it was a Volkswagen Beetle! Nobody was in it. There were tire tread tracks in the snow leading up to it. We had had a dusting of about one half inch of snow earlier in the morning.

The VW was parked in front of 1217 West 5th Street, a residence being rented by a couple whom we had previously arrested on drug charges. The home of Phil and Phyllis Ersberg was familiar to us in that they had moved there about five months before from an apartment they had rented on 4th Street across from the old Cathedral High School. It was at their old address where we had executed a search warrant resulting in their arrest.

After the Ersberg's court appearance, where they were sentenced to probation, they moved to the location at 1217 West 5th, and according to informants, were back in business.

Now, they were a case in study, He, Phil, was an independent radio and TV repairman of dubious sexual orientation, and Phyllis, a housewife, though not too much to brag about as a housekeeper. She was about five feet in height, and about the same in width. She had jowls that reminded you of Winston Churchill, or possibly Churchill's dog. She wore huge wire rimmed glasses that covered half her face. According to an informant, the kids who bought dope from her dubbed her, "Instant Gloom."

She surely did not fit the description of the dark haired female behind the wheel of the VW who had been waiting for and picked up the two suspects.

I parked about seventy five feet behind the VW, not wanting to be seen by anyone in the house, using nearby homes for cover.

I got out or our car, walked along the sidewalk and when I reached the VW, went to it's rear, bent over and felt the tailpipe. It was warm. Duluth's temperature was about 10 degrees Fahrenheit through most of the day..

A quick look through a window showed nothing more than a sweater and a couple of infant toys on the back seat. I noted for memory the license number and returned to our parked car.

Radich made a radio request for ownership of the VW, bearing Minnesota plates DJJ961.

At 1:17 P.M., Roger Armstrong, a Duluth Police/Fire Radio Communications Center Operator, passed on the Motor Vehicle Division listing for that vehicle: A 1971 Volkswagen Beetle, yellow, belonging to a Nancy A. Massey, 1207 East 5th Street, Duluth. We were familiar with Nancy and her sons. Their home was exactly 25 blocks east of the Ersbergs on 5th Street.

Nancy's sons had been among the broad list of possible suspects in a string of bank robberies which had spanned the past thirteen months.

As soon as Armstrong had completed his broadcast of the Massey listing, we got an excited call from one of the detective sergeants, Dick Yagoda, at the scene of the robbery. "Do you have that VW eyeballed now?"

"10-04," responded Radich.

"Where are you located?" was the next question.

"If you're at the bank, we'll call you by phone," Radich advised Yagoda.

Yagoda, wise veteran of many years of police work, instantly understood that we did not want to broadcast our location, which action would have brought every TV, radio and newspaper reporter to that scene. All the media and press have scanners.

We drove just over three blocks back to the direction from whence we came, and parked in front of a home. I went to the door, rang the bell and when a lady answered, showed my badge, identified myself and asked to use her phone for important police business. She quickly permitted entry to her home. I called the bank and spoke with Yagoda, advising him that the car was parked directly in front of the Ersberg's house. I also gave him a brief outline of our Narco Units involvement with them.

"Someone will come to where you guys are, in case you need a hand," Dick volunteered. "Be careful, these assholes are armed," he admonished. "You know the Massey boys, they are jerks who like to think they are big time, and they might try to put on a show if they're even at the Ersberg's now!"

'Thanks, Dick, we'll see you in a bit."

When we returned to near 1217 West 5th, the yellow VW was gone and tracks in the snow indicated that it had made a sharp U-turn from where it had been parked, facing west. We then called Yagoda via police radio and requested he send someone from the ID Unit to where we were to take photos of the tracks. We would preserve them until then.

While Rod moved our car into a position which would help save the tire tracks, I walked to the Ersberg house; it sat back about eighty feet from the street.

At the side door, I knocked and Phyllis Ersberg, aka "Instant Gloom" opened the door about fifteen inches.

Seeing me, she said, "What the hell do you want now, you son of a bitch? Have you got a search warrant?"

"What's there to be excited or paranoid about, Phyllis?" I asked. "I only want to know who the driver and passengers are to that yellow VW Beetle that was parked in front of your house until a few minutes ago?"

She calmed down a bit, "That was Yvonne Massey and her boyfriend John Murray."

I asked, "Were they visiting you?"

"No, they didn't visit, they had dropped off her two year old son, Elton, this morning and I've been babysitting him. They just stopped to check on him."

"What do you mean, did they just drop in to check on him or did they have something for him or you?" I asked.

She got huffy again. "Just what I said, they wanted to see him and then they said they forgot something, so they left. I don't know if they are going to come back today."

During this conversation, Instant Gloom was holding the door open by propping her immense body against it, keeping it from going any wider.

"Was anyone else with Yvonne and John when they were here?"

"No, now get the hell out of my house!"

Amused, I said, "Phyllis, if you will look very close, I'm standing outside your door, and you are blocking entry by me or anyone else with your petite body."

At just about that instant, I heard Radich shout in Yugoslavian, "Ilija, oni vrati," which means, "Eli, they're returning."

I jogged back toward the street in time to see Yvonne Massey park the yellow VW across the street, facing traffic.

Following a short distance behind, about two blocks, were two Duluth Police Department ID Techs in an unmarked car, Bob Gracek and Bob Cox, having been assigned to take photos of the tire tracks originally left by the VW on its first stop at that location. With them, was Steve Russell, fresh out of the FBI Academy and recently assigned to Duluth as his first post with the Bureau.

As Yvonne emerged from the drivers side, she went around the front and Agent Russell started to talk to her, but she ignored him and continued to walk across the street toward the Ersberg's.

I had walked around the rear of the VW and stopped by the driver's door.

"That's all right, Yvonne," I shouted, "We'll be calling a tow truck for your car, you're in violation, parked against the flow of traffic is a hazard if you try to pull out."

She stopped dead in her tracks and returned, but John Murray, her companion, continued on toward the Ersberg's house.

I quickly stepped in front of the VW driver's door to block her from opening the door with a key. "Too late, it's already been determined that a ticket is going to be issued and the car towed, we can't permit you to pull out against traffic in the wrong lane."

With that she started to pound on my chest with her doubled fists, shouting, "Get out of my way, you fucking pig!" She continued with that expression and a few other truck stop epithets, over and over.

She stood about five feet one and looked to weigh about one hundred pounds, a sprig of a thing, so her punches weren't too effective, and when I thought she might hear through her own shouting, I interjected, "That's really nice, Yvonne, now we've got your ass for assault on a police officer."

"Fuck you," she hollered, stopped pounding on me, and ran into the street heading for the Ersberg's house.

As she crossed the street, Agent Russell stepped in her way, spreading his arms, as if to stop her. As quick as a black belt in Karate, she kicked straight up toward his crotch and, because he immediately turned his hip to her, just missed his genitals. However, when turning his hip to her, he was off balance, so her kick did knock him three or four steps backward. Had it landed in it's original objective, Russell might have qualified for a disability pension early in his career.

Yvonne ran into the Ersberg's yard and into the house. No action was taken to restrain her, but officers were detailed to secure the home and prevent them from leaving.

A couple detectives who had arrived at the scene were briefed as to what had been learned and they were dispatched back to headquarters to prepare a search warrant for the VW Beetle.

They returned in less than an hour but would have even sooner if not for an ornery judge who would not see them until he had finished a conference with an attorney involved with a divorce case. Priorities? However, he did sign the warrant request authorizing the search. The officers also had asked him to be available for a search warrant for the Ersberg's house if we found probable cause to go further. He obstinately agreed, but said that they would have to find him at home, as he was going to call it a day early.

We opened the trunk latch to the VW. Inside we found four pieces of packed luggage. They were going on a trip.

In one of the smaller pieces was a small spiral notebook, with the first page outlining their agenda for the day:

8:30        A.M. Drop Elton off at Phyllis'

11:30 A.M.  Go to Arena Public Parking Lot. Look for the blue Ford pickup we had decided on. Jump wires and go.

12:00 P.M.  Park pickup east of North Shore Bank; wait for 5 minutes.

12:05 P.M.  Yvonne park on McCulloch Street in VW; Wait 8 but no more than 10 minutes, keep motor running

12:05 P.M. Carl and John go into North Shore Bank, do our thing

12:13/15      Dump pickup, leave with Yvonne

1:00 P.M.     Stop at Phyllis' pick up Elton. Give Phyllis $500.

              Go on vacation.


An urgent call was relayed through Radio Operator Armstrong to check if the district court judge has already gone home. He had, but one of the the other judges was just wrapping up his arraignments for the day and he said he would stick around until our officers got to his chambers. All other judges had cleared the courthouse long before. It was not quite three thirty P.M. Nice work if you can get it.

With agent Russell and Sergeant Tom Ehle, who had also responded to the scene, I went to the Ersberg's side door again and, when she answered, I advised her that we were getting a search warrant for her house, "But to save us time, and you the inconvenience, would you give us consent to search, sign a form, and we can start now."

"Screw all of you!" was her response, "you guys can stay out there and freeze your balls off as far as I care. I want you to show me a search warrant. I'm going to call my attorney about being harassed."

The temperature was a mild, January, ten degrees Fahrenheit.

"By all means," Sergeant Tom Ehle said, "call your lawyer."

When the search warrant arrived, I read it in its' entirety to Instant Gloom and our search team spread throughout the house.

The search produced an army field jacket with a two inch tear on the outside, lower left rear. It was found stuffed in a storm sewer pipe leading away from a catch basin, floor drain, in the basement.

Two pullover knit ski masks were found in the clothes washer, also in the basement. They were dry, and no other articles were in the washer.

The jacket and ski masks were impounded and inventoried.

John Murray and Yvonne Massey were placed under arrest for armed robbery of the North Shore Bank of Commerce and transported to the St. Louis County Jail by a couple of uniform officers who were assisting.

Phyllis Ersberg was advised that because she had her own two small children, as well as Yvonne's two year old, Elton, we were going to allow her to remain home, but that we would be requesting a warrant for her arrest for Conspiracy to Commit a Felony, bank robbery.

"I don't give a big fuck, all I was doing was babysitting, you got nothing on me," she said.

We knew that we had a good case against Yvonne and John but the remaining question was, who was the second male? The name Carl was mentioned in the notebook found in the trunk. One of Yvonne's brothers was named Carl.

Several bonuses were added later that day when, armed with a search warrant, a team led by SAIC Bob Harvey, went to John Murray's mother's home. He had maintained his old room with his mother at her home on South 58th Avenue West, and this was his legal residence.

The first bonus was an old army footlocker in John's bedroom. An architects sketch pad was found containing drawings of the floor plan for the North Shore Bank of

Commerce and floor plan sketches of five other banks which had been victims of robbery in the past thirteen months.

You might say that the drawings were almost to scale, except that reference to distance was in paces, not feet or yards. It was "eleven paces from front door to first tellers window: twenty three paces from front door to office door at rear of lobby."

Potted plants and pieces of lobby furniture were also identified and measurements given to each. They obviously had performed a thorough job of casing their targets.

Also found were a number of eight by eleven photos, black and white, of Yvonne and John, nude, in a variety of poses depicting sexual acts. In several photos, the camera was apparently held by a third person, but in most, they held the camera between them for close ups.

Among those photos, two showed Yvonne alone, lying on her back, nude, and performing a simulated sex act with a long barreled revolver. Most interesting, because letters and numbers could be seen on the side of the gun barrel, but they could not be totally identified.

The photos featuring the hand gun were rushed to a lab for enhancement, i.e, blowup, hopefully for identification of the letters and numbers on the barrel.

While we were awaiting the blowups of those photos, film developed from the banks security camera was delivered, also with blowups of the frames involving the long barreled revolver carried by one of the robbers. The brand name and serial numbers were clearly legible.

Toward evening the blowups of the photos from Murray's footlocker were returned. Brand name and serial number very legible and,——Bingo, a match.

Questioning Phyllis Ersberg the next day, FBI Agent Harvey impressed upon her the gravity of her involvement and she threw up all over Yvonne's brother, Carl. He was also indicted by a federal grand jury along with sister Yvonne and John Murray. Carl Massey was hiding behind the door 'Instant Gloom' had been holding on to when I first came to her door, armed with the long barrel revolver, and he had climbed out a back window before help arrived for us.

*Eli J. Miletich*

The trial took place in U.S. District Court in Duluth with Federal Judge Miles Lord presiding. The trial lasted four days and actually was pretty mundane, considering the preponderance of evidence, but it was not without some humor.

Nancy Massey, mother of Yvonne and Carl, and the owner of the get away car, sat in the front pew of the courtroom throughout the trial, appearing very menacing in a non feminine way, scowling throughout.

In recent years, Nancy had appeared to be very much involved in feminist, superwoman, and left wing causes, especially in the 70's. In doing so, it also appeared that she was encouraging her children that it was all right to "do your own thing" the philosophy of the so called beat or hippy generation.

As one who had been raised in an immigrant family, with parents who took their freedoms seriously, I was always involved in supporting candidates and issues which fit the mold that I favored, I.E., moderates who cared about economic and social justice, but I didn't include fringe, immoral causes in that bag.

With those opposing views, Nancy and I had crossed swords several times, at various community organizations and forums, on a variety of issues ranging from abortion, the legalization of certain controlled substances, and the decriminalization of homosexual acts.

When it came to my turn on the stand in the bank robbery trial, whenever I happened to glance in her direction, she, Nancy, mouthed expletives in my direction, inaudible, but even an amateur lip reader could see she was questioning the status of my parents at my birth and linking me to a member of the canine species.

Though what she was saying, inaudible as it was, couldn't be seen by anyone not looking directly out from the front of the courtroom, she did attract the attention of Judge Miles Lord. It was hard to keep from smiling or even laughing when, at one point the Judge, in noting her greetings to me, leaned over, covered his mouth partially and said, "I think she's in love with you."

After a short deliberation, the jury convicted both the Massey's and John Murray and they were sent away to a federal penitentiary.

Oh, by the way, Carol and Dana got their medication after midnight that night.

———————————

Over the next few years I had occasion to run into Federal Judge Miles Lord several times. One evening in particular, when on an assignment from Chief Tasky to check out an Oriental Rug auction for a potential scam, Rod Radich and I were in the Great Hall of the Radisson Hotel where hundreds of rugs were laid out on display, when we heard someone whisper, "What are Starsky and Hutch doing here?"

We turned around and there was the Judge in casual clothes, plaid shirt and khaki trousers.

I put my fingers to my mouth in a quick motion to let him know that we were checking the place out. He got the message and asked if he could tag along with us. How can you refuse a federal judge?

He did a great job though,playing a "rube" ready to buy any rug in the place. Just when the sales person thought he had this live one reeled in, the judge said, "Well, I think I had better go upstairs to my room and bring my wife down, I know she will like it and will want to buy it."

He gave us a wink and started for the lobby and we followed by a few seconds.

In the lobby, knowing that the judge lived in the Twin Cities area, I said, "Is your wife with you this trip, Judge?"

"No," he answered, "but the guy's high pressure sales would have had me pulling out my credit card in a short time if I didn't find a way to get out of there!" To this, we all had a good laugh.

Judge Lord told us that he was in town holding a trial on an embezzlement case but the defendant pled guilty before the trial was to start, so sentencing was to be the next day.

Even though the rug sales operation was a high pressure one, no crime was being committed, so Radich and I were going to return to our office, leave a report, punch out, and go to the "police officers hangout bar", the Pioneer, for a glass of beer before heading home. We asked the judge if he wanted to down a beer with us, and he genuinely seemed to appreciate the invitation.

He accompanied us to headquarters and browsed while we completed our paperwork. We then punched out.

At the Pioneer we indulged in a few beer and closed the place up at the one A.M. quitting time. It was nice to get to know the judge in an informal setting. He even took his turn at buying a round. Not a stuffed shirt or pretentious, pompous man, in robes or casual clothes.

An interesting footnote to this episode is that in 1982, when Mayor John Fedo sent my name to the city council for their approval, a hearing was set up, but prior to that hearing, Nancy joined several other "feminists" in sending a letter to the city council urging their rejection of me because I "wasn't sensitive to women's issues."

That hearing, conducted in a manner not too unlike a U.S. Senate confirmation hearing, was an opportunity for at least one left wing member of the council to echo some of the sentiments of those "feminists" in his cross examination of me with respect to my views on woman's rights, civil rights, etc.

Michael Paymar, that councillor, later moved to St. Paul, But

that too, is another story.

# Chapter Twenty

In January of '82, I received a call from Mayor John Fedo. "Are you busy?" he said.

"Damn right, I am always busy. You know that the taxpayers are always getting their moneys worth out of me." I cracked, knowing that he would be expecting such a remark from me.

"Bullshit," he said, "Come on upstairs, I'll buy you a cup of coffee, and I've got something I want to talk over with you,"

"Is the coffee lousy as usual? Give me about five minutes, I'm just wrapping up a report on our departments efforts to enforce the pornography ordinance in our fair city."

---

It needs to be said that as president of the Duluth Police Union, even though meetings with mayors' were adversarial at times, I had developed a good working relationship with all of the mayors for the previous seventeen years. Admittedly, in the long fight to establish collective bargaining rights for public employees, particularly police, I had tweaked a few noses and rubbed some people the wrong way.

Now the question of Administrative Assistant to the Mayor was another story, because I had a knack for being forthright with the man who had adeptly and mysteriously served four mayors over twenty years despite the fact that none of them were politically or philosophically close.

One mayor, Ben Boo, a good guy who had loads of managerial experience in government and with the Army Reserve, chose to delegate more to his AA than most mayors and it was during that administration that Clarence Maddy, the AA, assumed more authority than the City Charter had designated for that position. In effect, he was the de facto mayor.

I often said to him that he was a guy that if you asked him the time, he would look at the clock on the wall and tell you the name of the clock, that the face of the clock was white, the hands black, the second hand red, and every other irrelevant thing about the clock but not the time. So, when it came to negotiations, actually meet and confer, the guy spun wheels for countless hours then would wrap things up by claiming he had another meeting, and say

*Eli J. Miletich*

"Sorry fellows, but I can't agree to anything until I speak with the Mayor, but it doesn't look favorable." Arrogance it was and arrogance is the way I described it to him.

Before Minnesota had a Public Employees Labor Relations Law there were several of us in public safety circles around the state, among them Dick Fieder from the St. Paul Police Union, Roger Armstrong and Bob LaFlamme of the Duluth Firefighters Union, who envisioned a law providing for collective bargaining rights with respect to wages and terms and conditions of employment for public safety employees.

I had been so bold as to suggest that we carry that project to the two major political parties in the form of resolutions for their precinct caucuses, hopefully for progression all the way to their respective state conventions and, hopefully, approval as part of their party platforms, i.e., goals.

Roger Armstrong of the Firefighters liked the idea and together we drafted the resolution.

My wife,Carol, cut a stencil for an old hand rolled mimeograph machine. Copy machines were not available as yet. The machine was given to us by her brother, Bob

314

Peterson, who owned a Skelly service station and was about to sell his business and move to Rock Island, Illinois. About six dozen copies were made. Because we could not get too much support elsewhere, Roger and I and a handful of cops and firefighters attended the caucuses and failed miserably to get backing even on the local level. What we did not realize was that like other organizations that seek political support for their cause, or goals, we needed to really get members out in numbers to the caucuses. People sympathized with us, but they were not going to support resolutions that our own members were not present to lobby for.

Two years later, we were moderately successful by getting enough members to take part in caucuses on the Democratic side, but not with Republicans. Twice denied, but seeing support growing, we finally convinced cops and firefighters around the state to take part.

In 1971 both major parties approved resolutions calling for collective bargaining rights for public employees, with the right to strike in instances of impasse, except for public safety employees. Binding arbitration was the rule for us. We could live with that. At least we did not have to take the bones that Clarence Maddy tossed us so magnanimously when and if this were to become law.

Next, we needed to enlist the support of organized labor.

For years there was animosity between labor and police due largely to the misuse of police during those turbulent years in which private sector unions were attempting to organize and/or were conducting job actions such as legal strikes or slow downs.

Early on in my term as union president I had encouraged our members to become affiliated with the International Union of Police Associations, AFL-CIO, hopefully to reestablish a relationship with those organizations which had evaporated during the years of police repression against unions.

In Duluth, during the 20's and 30's, and even the 40's, police were utilized to invade peaceful picket lines with batons swinging, busting heads with glee, at the direction of their superiors who were kissing the butts of the industrial giants who controlled mining, lumber, shipping, steel making and the local newspaper.

One of the ugliest strikes in the history of the City of Duluth occurred back in the late thirties. Typesetters and printers were striking for the right to be recognized at the Duluth Herald and Duluth News Tribune, the city's morning and afternoon papers. Allegedly, the papers owners, the powerful Ridder family, asked city government to intercede. That intercession was in the form of helmeted club carrying police officers beating the living hell out of helpless picketers. Years later, I saw scores of telegrams of protest, in a file, which had been sent from all across the country over this outrage.

Another similar occurrence was the Seaman's Union strike in 1946 with the same police reaction.

But for the understanding and compassion of one man, Dave Roe, President of the Minnesota AFL-CIO, what we sought would have never come to pass. I'm sure that our membership in the AFL-CIO helped to frame his thinking a bit. We were the only police union in the state so affiliated.

As he acknowledged when testifying before state legislative committees on our behalf, "It is time to bury the hatchet with an important segment of working society. The labor busting goons of another day and era are not the fault or responsibility of our present day police officers, most of whom come from union families themselves.

To allow mayors, city managers and administrative assistants the unilateral, arbitrary discretion to set wages and conditions for these workers goes back to the dark ages.

Pass this legislation and allow them to have a voice in their future."

Sitting in the crowded hearing room at the capitol, I couldn't help but think that he was referring to our Administrative Assistant, Maddy, who enjoyed playing mind games, at times closing off a meeting by pointing out, "Under the Meet and Confer law, this is all that is required of me, meet and confer, nothing more."

We had to accept those crumbs and, in Duluth, police and fire employees were paid just a bit more than poverty level salaries.

The bill was passed and progress made by public safety employees since is history.

———————

When I got to Fedo's office he poured a cup of coffee for me and got right to the point.

"You know that Milo is retiring in May, don't you?" he asked.

"Sure," I answered, "everyone does."

It had been known for months that Milo Tasky, the present Police Chief, was reaching the mandatory retirement age of sixty five in May, and there was daily speculation as to who would succeed him.

"I've been reviewing names and files of possible candidates to fill that position, and I and my advisors have come up with a name and I want to know what you think of it."

My first thought was that he was going to throw out a name, possibly Ray Pound, for whom a not too subtle campaign had been started by left wing feminist groups, thereby checking my reaction as union president and how I might relate to that person. "Go ahead, who's the unlucky asshole?"

"You! Would you want to become a full time administrator and put some of your ideas into practice. I know that you have worked in all divisions of the Department and have some good proposals for consolidating positions and units to bring about some efficiencies in the overall operation, now will be your chance," he said.

In 1981, as a member of a City Hall task force set up to study and make recommendations for doing the job better, I had made several proposals for ridding the department of several of its paper shuffling positions and getting more people out on the street in patrol and investigations. My report to the main task force was well received but fell on deaf ears of the then department management.

"You know, Mayor, any cop worth a lick of salt is always dreaming about how he would do some things differently if he had a chance. You've got to remember, though, that I'm the guy who comes up here and argues with you at negotiation time; who brings unresolved grievances to your desk and, in general, raises hell on behalf of our membership. I've apparently done well by my union too, because despite the fact that I've moved upward in rank they've kept electing me as president. I'm flattered by your proposal."

"Look, I'm not looking for a yes man. If I wanted that, I know that I could find one. I really believe that you can do more for your department as Chief than in your present capacity as Lieutenant or for that matter, union president."

I'm not expecting that we won't have disagreements. That's the nature of both of us. When we do, we can argue them out. Sometimes I'll win and sometimes you will. I can assure you that I will never interfere with any matter of police policy. My concern as the elected administrator of the City will always be with all City department budgets, and I expect that we will have battles over that, but go ahead, prove me wrong," he concluded.

"If you're really serious, I accept, but what about Clarence Maddy, your Administrative Assistant?" I asked.

"Clancy's about to become history. As you know, he's been like a Rasputin, surviving through my three predecessors. I don't know how he did it, lasting twenty years. Must have had something on them," He laughed, "You would think he was Mayor. Anyway, I've asked for his resignation. I could fire him, but I decided to let him go in style. He's not happy, but I was the one elected to do this job, not him, and from day one he

*Eli J. Miletich*

has been trying to influence me the way he did the others before me."

"Where do I sign?" I asked, smiling broadly.

"I'll be sending a communication on your appointment to the City Council around the end of April, or the first of May. Keep it under your hat until then other than with your wife. Of course, the Council will have to hold hearings," he concluded.

"Any problems with me naming my own Assistant Chief?" I asked. "Fred's been doing a fine job, but I want Gene Sisto. You know that we've worked together in many capacities, grew up and played in the same neighborhood in fact. And I want someone who will watch my back."

"Only one other thing, I know the law draws a line between management rights and union rights, and I have no problem with that, but at least in our private meetings, you and I, I'll always support the wage requests by the union, that's my heritage."

"Okay with me," said Fedo.

"Thanks and, by the way, your coffee is lousy as usual, and cold too!"

322

"Jebi se." Were the words I heard from behind me as I went through the door. I had taught him that Croatian expression during other meetings over the previous two years.

## Chapter Twenty One

John Fedo is a politician with guts.

Back in the mid 1970's Fedo was a service station operator who fought a huge regional oil and gasoline supply corporation all by himself and won.

As a franchise holder of a Clark Service Station, he found that they had been making unreasonable demands on him which were not in the agreement between the two parties.

His one man revolt brought him some unintended notoriety and popularity.

When Fedo ran for city council, even though I did not know him, I supported him because of his tenacity in standing up to the big oil company and his displayed ability to speak publicly about his belief that the "little guy" needed someone in city government to speak up for him.

As a councillor, he sure did. His family background included a long tradition of backing Democratic-Farmer-Labor Party candidates, yet he maintained an independent posture, challenging the system when he saw it to be wrong. The system in Duluth and Northeastern Minnesota is D-F-L. He gained a great following and many supporters.

After a few years as a councillor, he decided to take on the incumbent Mayor, Bob Beaudin, a nice guy and friend of mine for years.

Beaudin was also a D-F-L'er, and one who usually toed the party line, so he was a favorite of the party officers, "bosses", as they're referred to in other parts of the country. These are the folks, never elected to public office, but who have as much, maybe more, clout than anyone holding office. They get their way with a simple phone call more often than not.

The primary election was in September of 1979, and my vote went to long time friend, Beaudin. John Fedo won the primary against Beaudin and a former mayor, Ben Boo, with Boo placing second, thus facing off with Fedo in November. Fedo, having built himself a strong populist constituency, handily defeated Boo.

A new, young and vibrant, city government took office in January, 1980.

With a strong program designed to lift a city up from what, in fact, was a twenty year recession, Fedo went after federal and state funds as no mayor before him, He pounded on tables and tweaked noses. He presented a budget with no new local taxes.

Unexpended Interstate Freeway dollars were fought for and, when allocated, put to renovation and redevelopment projects throughout the city. A dark foreboding downtown was converted almost overnight into a mecca for tourism.

New industry and business were solicited to build in the city.

With matching funds, existing businesses were encouraged to remodel and clean up their storefronts. Heated Skywalks, connecting buildings, coursed the entire downtown including City Hall and the St. Louis County Courthouse.

Parks, long neglected under previous administrations, were given high priority. Overgrown with weeds and brush, they had become a haven for drunks and drifters.(Note. Duluth is reported to have more parks and playgrounds than any mid sized U. S. city).

On the downtown waterfront, a Lake Walk about two miles long was constructed, drawing thousands of tourists as well as residents, to the shore throughout the year to admire the grandeur and beauty of Duluth and Lake Superior.

When he heard of a possible intent on the part of a major airline to seek a new location for a needed maintenance facility for its new Airbus line of airplane, he went after it ferociously. In fact, Al Chechi, the board chairman of that airline, Northwest, at the time of the announcement that Duluth had been selected, said that he was glad that they had finally made the decision to pick Duluth, "because mayor Fedo, when he gets hold of your ankle, hangs on like a bulldog and won't let go until you've picked his city!"

The finding of good paying, long term jobs was Fedo's goal, and achieve that goal he did.

It is noteworthy that cities which were in competition with Duluth for this huge project are major hubs in the Northwest Airlines system: Minneapolis, Detroit, Memphis, Kansas City and Seattle.

Someone once told me that there is an axiom in politics that if you do nothing, or very little, you are always Mr. Nice Guy, and people will always say nice things about you.

It follows that if you are a leader with vision and dedication, sometimes finding it necessary to get tough with naysayers and status quo devotees, you are going to develop, not by design, a cult of opposition to your incumbency, in fact, to your very being. I also found that to be true as a police administrator.

So it was with Mayor John Fedo.

Fedo was reelected in 1983 with token opposition put forth by the political establishment. He continued with his assertive program of preparing the city for the twenty first century.

In 1987 the party bosses joined forces with some of the downtown power brokers and university intelligentsia in backing a candidate they hoped would get rid of a mayor whom they thought had become more powerful than themselves.

Stories started to circulate in coffee shops and beauty parlors about alleged personal flaws in Fedo's character: He was deep in debt; never paid his bills; was a wife beater and too many others to recount here. A well oiled character assassination by innuendo and rumor, was the method of attack in as much as they surely could not go after his record which was loaded with accomplishments.

It's with that background scenario that several months later I got a phone call from the County Attorney.

One day in October, the 7th to be exact, apparently after they believed they had sufficiently saturated the community with Nixon like dirty tricks, Alan Mitchell called me.

"Hi Chief," he said, "we've got something very important to talk over with you. Would you be able to come to my office in about an hour?"

"What about, Al," I asked, "if it's an investigation our guys are working on, why don't I just send over the Inspector of the Detective Bureau?"

"No, it's more important than that, and we need to talk with you about it."

"Okay, I'll try to make it over to the Courthouse around one thirty."

When Al Mitchell ran for the office of St. Louis County Attorney in the mid seventies, he was a very young and relatively unknown, untried, attorney who in the September primary ran against a field of more experienced attorneys, four in all, who were challenging the incumbent, a personable but overrated guy by the name of Brownell who's office set records for plea bargaining.

Because I knew Mitchell as a young kid from my western Duluth community, and more importantly, because our families had been friends for many years and they are good people, I decided to support him.

Being president of the Duluth Police Union and admittedly an activist, I sought endorsement of our body for Mitchell and gained approval. We were the first organization to back him. Shortly thereafter, at the regional quarterly meeting of the Arrowhead Police and Peace Officers Association, we won area wide endorsement for him by the delegates in attendance. His candidacy had gained some important momentum.

As I have said, I have always enjoyed politics as a hobby, supporting some winners as well as losers. This was the worst political choice I had ever made!

Mitchell won the primary and the general election. One wheeler-dealer was replaced by another of the same mold, a little more laid back and less flamboyant, but no less prone to playing ball with the power brokers. As the legal counsel for the County Board, he soon assumed a Rasputin like persona with that generally incompetent elected body.

---

On August 31, 1982, several months after I had been appointed to the Police Chief position, an ugly incident occurred in the hillside neighborhood above the downtown of Duluth, a neighborhood which would be labeled 'center city' in similar cities elsewhere.

A biracial couple living at 132 East 5th Street, sharing an apartment with another couple, was confronted around midnight by a small gang. Several bikers and hangers on gathered outside their home, shouting racial taunts and epithets as well as verbal treats, challenging the folks inside to come out.

When the couple refused to show themselves, the crowd assembled a crudely made cross from a couple four by fours, doused it with kerosene, stood it up upright into a hole already dug in the ground and set it ablaze. Shades of Ku Klux Klan.

The frightened young couple, and their friends, phoned another friend to come pick them up in a car.

When that friend pulled his car up to the curb, the four tenants ran from the apartment and jumped into the waiting car. However, before they could speed off, the vandals broke all the windows by swinging heavy chains at the car.

Police squads responded to calls from neighbors and when they arrived at the scene, naturally the idiot bikers were gone, but the officers were able to get the names of the two key ringleaders from several observers in the crowd.

The next morning, after reviewing the Incident Reports as submitted by all units from the previous days activities, including the cross burning, I noted that the officers had requested warrants for felony counts on the suspects whose names witnesses had furnished.

I called Detective Inspector Ernie Grams and asked him if the reports had been submitted to the County Attorneys office as yet for prosecution under Minnesota's Terroristic Threats Statute.

"They've already sent the file back with instructions to send the reports to the City Attorney's office for prosecutions as misdemeanor offense, in other words, Disturbing the Peace," Said Grams.

"Hold off on that, Inspector, I think that we have something more than a simple Disturbing the Peace or Disorderly Conduct here. We can't let Mitchell get by with this," I said. "Call the County Attorney's office and advise them that I have read the statute with reference to Terroristic Threats and I agree with the officers who investigated the incident. The statute applies in this case!"

About a half hour later Grams called. "Alan Mitchell says that he is not going to have any police chief tell him how to run his office. He's adamant. They will not prosecute."

"Fine," I said, "I'm not trying to run his office, but we have a city to protect, and that asshole doesn't manage this department. I can see if an incident like this is treated lightly it has the potential to escalate. We're not going to stand by idly while he twiddles his thumbs. You can call him one more time and advise him that I will be having a press conference this afternoon and will be making copies of the squad officers reports available to the press and media."

Shortly before noon Dolores Pohjola, my secretary, buzzed me. "The County Attorney is on the line, do you want to talk with him?"

"You bet."

"Chief, I'm just calling to let you know that, against my better judgment, we're going to try those guys under the Terroristic Threats Statute, but I think it's a weak case. Further, I'm not going to be pressured by City politics to have anyone on my staff do something that I don't feel comfortable about, so I'm going to handle the prosecution myself. Mind you, I think we're going to lose," he said.

I had only said hello initially before he went into his diatribe, so when I did get a chance to say something, I lit into him.

"Al, I don't give a shit if your office prosecutes this case or not. There are no city politics involved here. The officers at the scene did a thorough job in collecting evidence and obtaining victim and witness statements. It's their belief that the Terroristic Threats Statute applies and I support that. We just can't have that crap going on in this city. If you don't have the guts to follow up on this, don't do me any favors. Just forget it, and we'll let the public know what's going on. I'll tell you another thing, I've got photos of the June 15, 1920 incident in the files in this office and it's exactly the kind of apathy which you show now that allowed that lynching to happen!"

"That's not a fair comparison. This was just an act of vandalism."

"Bullshit, like I said, you don't have to prosecute!"

"I said we were going to prosecute, but I won't promise any convictions."

"Fine," I said, "have a good day."

"Goodbye," he closed.

Prior to trial the African-American who was one of the targets of the terrorism was further victimized by several anonymous phone threats and was subsequently advising investigators that he was not going to testify no matter how much cajoling and pleading was applied. Because I knew a friend of the family, I decided to involve myself and called the young man's mother and asked her to bring him in for a meeting. Somehow, between his mom and me, we were able to change his mind.

The two suspects were tried separately with Mitchell handling the prosecution himself.

The first to be prosecuted was convicted and sentenced to three to five years in a state pen. Expert police work and good witness testimony got the results on this one.

The trial of the second subject was declared a mistrial, not because of any police error, but due to Mitchell's mishandling the questioning of a police witness. The presiding judge, Jack Litman, disturbed by Mitchell's presentation of the case, had pertinent segments of the trial transcribed and sent to me in the event I wanted to challenge Mitchell for his shoddy job.

He, Mitchell, was a bit under the gun to retry, however, due to the conviction of the first subject, so he went for a new trial. A conviction resulted with the same sentence.

Though the County Attorney himself does not usually try criminal cases, he has a staff of prosecutors for that, to my recollection these are the only two felony cases that our esteemed County Attorney has tried himself since his original election. His batting average is 1,000 per cent. Ironic, since he was adamantly opposed to charging them with felonies, instead, wanting the City Attorney to charge them with Misdemeanors, expressing his belief that he would not win.

It could be that the mention of the June 1920 lynching may have got him off his dead rear end!

---

On the night of June 14, 1920, a young unmarried couple, both white, went to a carnival which had been set up for ten days in the large field to the southwest of the Duluth Dukes professional team's home field, Athletic Park.

As they walked around the midway, they passed a group of loitering carnival workers, all black, and according to later investigation, heard some wisecracks with sexual innuendo mixed in. The young man wanted to challenge the loudest of the group, but his girlfriend urged him not to, and she prevailed.

The couple left the carnival shortly thereafter walking hand and hand through a field on the outskirts of the carnival. As they walked they became cozy with each other and lust overcame them. They went to a secluded spot and engaged in sex.

The young man walked his girlfriend home and she found her mother waiting up for her. It was after midnight and her mom noticed grass stains on the daughters clothing, further

338

that her hair was all disheveled with straw dangling from it. Her mom immediately questioned her about her activities during the evening.

The girl, not wanting to admit intimacy with her boyfriend, said, "Three black carnival workers raped me." That statement set off a chain of events which culminated in one of the most disgraceful incidents in the history of Duluth.

When the father, who had been to a pool hall in West Duluth for the evening came home, he quickly went down to the West Duluth police precinct and they in turn called headquarters downtown.

As it turned out, the carnival had already torn down their tents and sideshows, packed everything on a train and were heading for Virginia, Minnesota, in the Iron Range mining country about sixty miles north of Duluth. Police found out that the train had to hook up to another engine at a junction in Carlton, a town about twenty two miles west of Duluth.

The police reaction was swift and they took several cars and drove to Carlton meeting up with the train before it got underway again.

With the description offered by the girl, height, approximate weight and clothing, the police picked out the three likely suspects, placed them under arrest and brought them back to the city jail, then located on Superior Street between 1st and 2nd Avenue East.

Back in the West Duluth neighborhood, when news of the arrests reached the pool halls and speakeasies, a mood started to develop. "We can't let those guys come to town and do that to our young women," was repeated over and over again.

By mid afternoon the next day, groups had gathered along Central Avenue and Grand Avenue, West Duluth's two main business thoroughfares, and before long someone shouted, "Let's go downtown and make sure those niggers pay for their crime!" That started it.

Trucks jammed with men, cars filled with men standing on the running boards, horses pulling wagons loaded with drunks carrying axe handles and hundreds on foot slowly started off from the intersection of Grand and Central. Estimated at about two thousand and growing like a ball rolled to make a snowman, the crowd gathered momentum as it passed through different neighborhoods.

As it, now a mob, crawled through the West End, it grew to three thousand, and by the time they reached Little Italy, four thousand. When it reached the front of police headquarters which also housed the jail, it was believed to be over five thousand.

Chants of racial epithets engulfed the air demanding that the police turn over the prisoners to the mob.

The harried police on duty at headquarters made calls to city hall. Oddly enough, the Mayor was out of town and none of the city council was available. The mob grew with every passing half hour.

The Sergeant on duty as Officer in Charge that evening made a call to the Fire Department when stones started coming through the windows. He talked to an Assistant Chief. "Can you send a few guys down here with hoses, we've got a big mob out front, and I'm afraid they are going to ram down the door to Headquarters. If we can turn a hose on them and get them wet, it might help break it up?" he asked in desperation.

"There's no way I am going to send my men down there, that's a police problem, not a fire matter."

No police supervisors were around, nor could any be found at their homes, at least that is what their wives claimed. The Chief of Police and two of his Captains had left earlier in the afternoon for Virginia, allegedly to pick up two more suspects whom the Virginia police had taken into custody from the carnival when it arrived in that city. Odd that some sergeants or patrolmen were not assigned that detail? Of an approximate one hundred twenty man department, only the sergeant and five of his men were there to withstand the mob for over five hours. It, the mob, had now grown to over ten thousand.

The Fire Department Assistant Chief apparently had a change of heart and a crew of firefighters finally showed up, tried to hook up their hoses to nearby hydrants, but the mob overcame them, took the hoses away and scattered the firefighters. Then it happened.

With battering rams made of old telephone poles and railroad ties, they knocked down the doors, rushed in, beat up the police with fists and pick axe handles and took the keys to the cell block. They ran up and down the aisles checking each cell until they found two young black males cringing in the corner of their respective cells.

As they were dragging them out, someone noticed the third one missing and shouted, "Hey, where's the third one?"

Back in went a large group and in checking the cell block more thoroughly this time, they found him in the dark shadow of the bunk in his cell. He was wearing a black shirt and pants and almost got away with it.

The three were promptly taken exactly one block up the hill to 2nd Avenue East and 1st Street, ropes looped around their necks and the loose ends of the ropes thrown across the telephone pole cross bar. The mob closest to the ropes began pulling until they were each dangling about five feet above the ground. The mob looked on for a while, posed for several photos, and dispersed.

One of the nations last, if not *the* last, racial lynching had occurred in the northern city of Duluth, Minnesota on June 15, 1920.

Eli J. Miletich

Under intensive police questioning after the fact, the girl and boy admitted to their own inappropriate behavior and she, to her lie.

A grand jury was assembled to try to deal with the lynching, attempting to pursue at least those who had been identified as the ringleaders. Of three for whom indictments were sought, two were dismissed for lack of sufficient evidence, but one was charged with inciting a riot and murder. A jury trial found him not guilty.

The three innocent victims were given a private Christian burial by a minister from the First Lutheran Church who also feared for his own safety for doing so. They lay in anonymous, unmarked, graves in a local cemetery for seventy one years.

In the fall of 1991, a public memorial service was held at the cemetery where the lynching victims had been buried.

Several days prior to that ceremony, Odie Powell, the City of Duluth Equal Opportunity Officer, came into my office for a scheduled meeting about our efforts at minority recruiting and, in passing, mentioned the upcoming ceremony at the cemetery.

'Would you be interested in going?" he asked. Odie just happens to be African American and a good friend.

"Sure, I'll drive and you can ride with me if you want."

During the service in which new headstone monuments would also be dedicated, one of the clergy, a minister from the modern day First Lutheran Church was speaking and, in his comments stated something to the effect that with this ceremony involving people of all races, "We pray that their souls would now be free of doubt and will soar to heaven as on wings of an eagle."

A little old woman standing next to me nudged me in the hip with her elbow and pointed skyward. About three hundred feet above the cemetery there was a beautiful white headed American Eagle, doing circles, soaring above the crowd gathered below.

I poked Odie and after he looked up he in turn did the same to the person standing next to him until about one half of the group of around five hundred were looking to the sky.

The folks, clergy and dignitaries, involved in the ceremony were under an open sided tent which had been set up earlier in

*Eli J. Miletich*

case of inclement weather. They had no way of knowing what was going on. The minister finished his comments.

When I looked up again, the eagle was gone and the program was concluded. Cecil B. DeMille, in his great Hollywood Biblical movies couldn't have arranged for a more dramatic finale.

Chapter Twenty Three

At 1:30 P.M. I arrived at County Attorney Mitchell's office and was ushered into one of his assistants office for the meeting he had asked me to attend.

Assistant's John DeSanto and Mark Rubin were seated on chairs set in a semi circle, with Mitchell himself seated behind the desk.

The one chair left for me was set apart from the rest, almost as if I was about to be interviewed, or better yet, interrogated.

I slid that chair over about four feet so that it was butting up against the desk, thus making my position in the room part of that semi circle, more like a meeting or conference setting than the aforesaid interrogation.

"I'll get to the point right away, Chief. What we wanted to talk with you about is a complaint that I received that Mayor Fedo has been submitting vouchers for expenses which he has never incurred. In other words, false claims for which he has received reimbursement from the City Treasurer," said Mitchell.

"You've lost me, what in hell are you talking about?" I asked, puzzled.

"This, I have met with two complainants, at a local bar, who say that they can attest to the fact that they are listed on expense vouchers submitted by Mayor Fedo for meals while attending meetings with legislators at the Capitol in St. Paul. Their statement is that they never were in attendance at such and such place and meeting. Thus, how can the Mayor claim that he picked up the expense for their dinner or lunch? They say that these false claims have occurred a number of times and that they want him held to account for this by criminal charges," explained Mitchell.

"Al, this has to be the frosting on the cake," I said, "you have to be aware of the multitude of rumors which have been going around with the election only one month away. This sure smells like politics at its worst. I know, as well as the whole city knows, that Fedo has been spending a lot of time at the capitol in St. Paul, lobbying for appropriations for a new convention center as well as for expansion of the zoo and some new facilities for the campus at the University of Minnesota, UMD, here in Duluth.

I also know that he's not getting much help in his efforts from our city representatives in the legislature because he has been upstaging them. Matter of fact, several of them are opposing his effort to bring those projects to fruition.

I would guess that, like anyone else lobbying those freeloading legislators, he doesn't get to meet with them other than over a meal for which he gets to pick up the tab. Also, they then pocket their per diem meal expense that legislators receive. And, by the way, since when do you or anyone on your staff meet with complainants in a bar and not your office?"

"You may want to downplay this Eli," he interjected, "but we have to take these complaints seriously. I want to know what you feel about an investigation. Do you think that your department should handle this? Do you feel that with the Mayor as the elected administrative head of the City, your department can do an unbiased or unintimidated investigation?"

"You're damned right we can do a thorough, unintimidated, unbiased investigation, regardless of who the subject is," I said,

349

"but I get the sense that this meeting was set up to be an exercise at intimidation itself. You know me better than that!

You said that you have two complainants, have you checked them out for possible motives, what with this being the political season, rather than running into this like a bull in a China Shop?

And when you asked if my department can do this investigation unbiased or unintimidated, you are casting aspersions on my integrity and I resent that.

My record shows that I run a clean ship. I have disciplined, nay, punished, several of my best friends on the department who have erred.

As you are well aware, I even took action to prosecute and terminate the employment of a good friend who, coincidentally, saved my life once!"

"Don't get all in a big huff now, Chief, I'm not questioning your integrity, I'm just letting you know what we have here, and I'm seeking your input. I know that it's a touchy subject, what with Fedo being the guy who appointed you and is your boss, but we know that you are an honest cop first."

Settled down a bit, I said, "Boss or no boss, from what you have explained thus far, I'm of the opinion that this is but another in a series of political dirty tricks designed to get the voters mad at the guy. I know that we could handle this properly, but my recommendation to you is that you bring in an outside investigatory agency which will have no connection to local government whatsoever.

I don't want our guys to work this, nor do I suggest that you have the Sheriff's staff do it. The political bias of your friend the Sheriff, who you helped to get elected, could tend to color any effort by that department."

"Who do you suggest then?" asked Mitchell.

"Well, if you are hell bent for leather on this, I'd suggest the Minnesota Bureau of Criminal Apprehension, BCA. They have a staff of skilled and experienced investigators. But, let me be honest with you. From what you have given me thus far, it still smacks of politics. In other words, you don't have shit!" I said with emphasis.

During the entire session neither DeSanto or Rubin said much other than to echo several comments made by Mitchell, their boss.

When I stood to leave, we shook hands all around and Mitchell asked me to keep our conversation confidential until, if and when, an investigation got underway. I assured him of that and left.

Upon my return to my office, I removed the miniature tape recorder which I had in my suit coat pocket. I listened to the tape to be sure that I captured the conversation in its entirety. It was all there. I saved the tape for posterity.

One week later County Attorney Mitchell announced that his office had requested the BCA to conduct an investigation of alleged criminal false claims for reimbursement on the part of Mayor John Fedo. Further, that the investigation would not get underway until after the election in November. Their hope, obviously, was to influence the outcome of the election. The local newspaper, the Duluth News Tribune, a Fedo enemy, loved it.

John Fedo won reelection to a third four year term by a wide margin.

Not to be deterred, County Attorney Alan Mitchell took the results of a not too conclusive BCA investigation, called a Grand Jury into session and through a mousy assistant prosecutor, spoon fed that body bits of information; brought his two complainants, a state senator and a lobbyist from Duluth, before the Grand Jury where, with half truths, they convinced the Grand Jury that there was at least enough probable cause to bring Fedo to trial.

As we know, a Grand Jury's deliberations and the entire proceedings are supposed to remain secret, but someone intentionally let out bits and pieces to the press and media, apparently expecting to sway the thinking of any potential future trial jury members.

The trial lasted several weeks. The testimony of prosecution witnesses was very weak. No physical evidence was presented to indicate any wrongdoing. John Fedo was acquitted and exonerated of all charges.

The bosses had been beaten!

353

Ironically, Mitchell's two complainants, a state senator and lobbyist, became targets of a statewide investigation, several years later, into illegal use of state property, i.e., thousands of dollars in long distance phone calls by cronies, in a case which the media in the Twin Cities dubbed "Phonegate". The subjects made public apologies for their "indiscretion", and made restitution. Neither County Attorney Mitchell nor then State Attorney General Hubert Humphrey III took any legal action to prosecute?

Chapter Twenty Three

## October 8

In the morning, Bob Harvey called the FBI office in San Diego and found that they were not too interested in getting involved by interviewing Smith's parents. They had to be prodded. Alexander suggested that Harvey call a regional supervisor. He did.

A result was that they learned that Michael Smith was their son. Vukovich was an alias. Michael Smith had a criminal record that included charges of robbery, burglary, theft, false imprisonment and possession of narcotics with intent to sell. San Diego PD was also interested in talking with him about a couple homicides, apparently drug related, done execution style.

With a positive ID on Michael Smith, Alexander compiled a thick file for prosecutors, thus a criminal complaint was issued in District Court in Duluth charging him with second degree homicide.

*Eli J. Miletich*

That evening Lieutenant Bev Ecklund made an undercover call to the Smith family. "Hi, this is Nancy, from Minneapolis, a friend of Mike's, could I talk to him?'

"He's not home right now," replied a womans voice, "the last time we heard from him he called from Detroit, he's a seaman you know, and he said he was heading for the East Coast to see if he can find a job on a seagoing merchant ship. Can I take a message?"

"No, I'm sure he will call me before his ship leaves port, he always does. Thank you, anyway," said Bev.

Harvey had learned from the San Diego FBI that Smith had done the same thing, shipped out, a year before when a man he knew was gunned down and then stabbed to death.

The bulletin and accompanying photo and sketch of Michael Smith were now circulated to most cities and towns on the East Coast.

A skillful act of diplomacy and tact on the part of the San Diego FBI led the Smith family to cooperate with them and a tracer was put on their phone on a possibility that son Michael might call again before shipping out.

Alexander and Inspector Sowl came in to my office to brief me on the status of the case up to that point.

"Notwithstanding their hesitancy this morning, we've sure been getting tremendous cooperation from the FBI and all other law enforcement agencies while trying to put this puzzle together," said Fred, "with just a few exceptions over the years, the level of cooperation with the feds has usually been good and we don't have any pompous agents talking down their nose at us. They've had some very dedicated guys assigned here and they realize that we have a competent department."

I agreed with Fred, "And those exceptions, while a nuisance, haven't diminished the common goal of putting crooks in jail, even though we have to kick the feds in the ass once in a while."

———————————

There was situation, a few years back, when Mike Anderson was working an informant on a case involving the theft and transfer out of state of a large amount of weapons.

The distributor was located in Two Harbors, a small town, also on Lake Superior, about twenty miles north of Duluth and our guy, Anderson, was assigned to the Narcotics-Vice Unit at that time. The informant was telling him that the target suspect was selling hot guns as well as drugs. Mike had carried the weapons thing as far as he could, so when he asked me about it, I suggested he contact the Alcohol, Tobacco and Firearms office, known as the ATF, of which the nearest unit was in Minneapolis.

Anderson made contact and they sent up a guy who we never felt comfortable with, a hot dog. His name was John Magarac, a first class donkey.

On one previous case which we had tuned him in on, he tried to induce our informant to give him information exclusively, thus cutting us off, in other words, stealing our snitch. A no no in law enforcement. We filed this in our memory bank.

After receiving a verbal briefing from Anderson, he, Magarac, got copies of all of the reports from our files from which Mike very carefully blacked out any allusion to the informant or his location.

"Can I have your informants name so I can debrief him myself?" he asked.

Mike told him that in as much as this informant was still working on active cases with our department, it was not possible, as we did not want him burned. He seemed to accept that. One of our other investigators continued to assist him in the gun investigation, even though the alleged offense had occurred outside our jurisdiction.

Arrests were subsequently made, and when the ATF forwarded Magarac's summary report to us for our files, we received a mild shock.

He, Magarac, had not mentioned the fact that the initial, in fact majority, information on the case had come from the Duluth PD. Rather, in an unabashed effort to ingratiate himself with his superiors, he started off his report like this: "*While working an informant in the Duluth, Minnesota area, I developed information which led me to believe that there was probable cause to believe that a suspect who lives approximately twenty miles north of Duluth, may be trafficking in stolen weapons———————.*"

*Eli J. Miletich*

Needless to say, Mr. Magarac became persona non grata in the Narcotics-Vice Unit of the Duluth PD. I had apprised our superiors of his shenanigans and they concurred.

In my experience, other than guys like Robbie Williams, who was working out of the Eau Claire, Wisconsin office of the ATF, and a few others like him, that federal agency is staffed with untested personnel. People who went to work with that agency, in general, had no blisters on their hands. In other words, they come fresh out of college, or from work as a clerk in a shopping mall, or some such occupation. Never having had to work with their backs or hands, they could not understand the nature and sensitivities of people who do so, and in many instances are hot dogs, i.e., know it all, did it all, but don't know how to deal with people problems.

One thing you will always see in a good experienced cop is teamwork. Getting the job done properly and objectively is paramount. As a wise old cop once said, "Mistaken once in a while, but never in doubt." Never did figure out what he meant by that.

## October 11

A few more days went by with no word on Smith, aka Vukovich.

On the afternoon of October 11th, Fred Sowl called and gave me an update.

"As a result of the tracer on the Smith phone line, San Diego FBI agents learned that Michael Smith had been in Cleveland, that he was going to an unidentified small town in upper New York state and would be staying there for a day or so, was then going to sign on as a seaman on a merchant ship.

Apparently he had another female who had put him up for a while. He told his parents that he would call them when he arrived at his destination, and before he ships out," said Sowl.

Bob Harvey also brought in copies of Smith's rap sheet which his FBI buddies faxed him from San Diego.

"The guys track record was loaded with charges of drugs and violence. His regular companions are suspected drug dealers and there is some suspicion that they play hardball when it comes to enforcing their particular code of silence.

Their cocaine connections are believed to be involved with the Medellin Cartel out of Colombia, South America. At the least, several unsolved homicides could be connected to them."

I said, "Thanks Fred, I think our guys are doing a top notch job, we'll get this guy."

As I hung up the phone, Sergeant Alexander came in and advised that he was being assisted by Hall and Ecklund in putting together a voluminous case file to be used by prosecutors after the apprehension of Smith. "I think that the teamwork we're seeing on this case is a classic example of police work at its best," he said. "The help we're getting from Harvey and the FBI, the Indianapolis PD and the other law enforcement agencies is staggering. It makes a guy feel good to know that there are people out there who care and can do this kind of work."

"Pat, you know what I always say about spinning wheels. You got to push sometimes to get out of a deep snow drift. In some ways, police work is like that, you got to push, cajole, encourage and praise people, and if you do, things will come together most of the time. It looks like you're doing that with this case and it is coming along. Keep it up.

By the way, when Fred just told me about this Smith's possible Colombian connections, it reminds me of a couple cases we initiated and worked on together involving Duluth dopers with Colombian ties which brought about some great results."

---

*How can you tell when a lawyers is lying?*

Here's another lawyer tale. One of a corrupt, lying jerk who works from both inside and outside the system.

In the early eighties, an informant made contact with Denny Lepak in the Narco-Vice Unit with information that three guys from Duluth were on their way from Duluth to Miami where they would spend a couple days negotiating with some Colombians. If things worked out in their favor, in other words a price agreed on, they would catch a flight to Bogota to complete arrangements of a quantity of cocaine.

Marc Vasler, Finley Douglas and Merdy Thomas were known to police officers in the area as small time. In their early twenties, all had led nondescript lives, though Thomas was one of the outstanding high school soccer players of his time.

Most of the intelligence information on them was that they were users of grass and that, once in a while, they dabbled in LSD and that they were always trying to make a big score.

The informant was tight enough with the three suspects that we were even able to obtain their arrival time in Miami on the flight from the Minneapolis-St. Paul International Airport. Their tentative departure to Bogota was likewise supplied.

With that solid information, Ron Swanson, Drug Enforcement Agency Special Agent in Charge in Duluth was contacted by Pat Alexander.

Swanson came into our office and we gave him the complete rundown on the three Colombia bound suspects. Swanson in turn returned to his office and plugged the pertinent info into the DEA's computer system, alerting, in particular, the offices responsible for monitoring the ports of embarkation in Miami, New Orleans and Houston. Thus, when they left Miami, they were bid farewell by several unseen agents who would also await their return.

After spending several days roaming aimlessly around Bogota, drinking, smoking hashish and seeing what locals they could bed, things got serious.

Marc Vasler was gone from their room when they woke up on the morning of the fourth day of their stay. When he returned, about mid afternoon, he told them that he had made contact with the source, a Colombian from the town of Cartagena, and that delivery of their cocaine would take place in San Juan, Puerto Rico.

When questioned by his partners about why they did not get invited to meet with the Colombian, Vasler told them that the Colombian wanted to limit the number of people he dealt with for reasons of security, and that if he, Vasler, told them anything about the man, his life would be in danger. They understood.

Vasler then told them that he had coincidentally met a girl he knew from Minneapolis, first name Lacy, who was visiting in Bogota. He said that they had snorted a bit of coke that afternoon and that she was going to return to the states when they did, and she agreed to go to San Juan with them. When she returned to Miami, she was going to smuggle a one pound glassine bag of cocaine back to mainland U.S. in her vagina.

The next couple days they partied, going from Bogota to Medellin to Cartagena and back to Bogota. Coke and sex were the menu for each day.

Somewhere during that time of partying the girl, Lacy, met up with a guy from St. Paul, had gone to shack up with him and didn't return. Vasler figured that she ditched them. So what, he thought, back in Duluth there are a couple others who will carry out the same mission if he calls on them.

Back in Bogota Vasler had contacted the airlines and changed their departure date and flight three different times, the last time even changing the place of departure from Bogota to Barranguilla. Apparently, his paranoia had convinced him to use such tactics to throw any surveillance off track.

When the adventurers arrived in Miami on the evening of February 5th, Vasler and Douglas were strip- searched by U.S. Customs. Both were clean, but Vasler was found to be carrying over eight thousand dollars in cash in a money belt fastened around his waist. No crime to be carrying money, but he was grilled about carrying that kind of cash and he told them that he was in Colombia looking for artifacts and antiques, but struck out, finding none.The agents seemed to accept that.

They checked into a Miami Airport hotel for the night.

Vasler had to talk way into the night to convince his partners that the way they were handling the delivery of the cocaine was the safest.

He explained that since Puerto Rico was a territory of the United States, when they left San Juan to return to the States, they would not be going through Customs, that it was like going from one state to another on the mainland. They finally agreed to follow through with Vaslers plan.

Finley Douglas and Merdy Thomas, motivated by greed, thinking about the big split they would receive at the end of this journey, let their fear of being caught be overcome by their love of dollars they did not have to labor for. Also, it was nice traveling with Vasler as long as he was picking up the tab for flight, room and meals. "Like a vacation." said Douglas, with a growing knot in his stomach.

On February 6th, the three conspirators checked out of the hotel, went directly to the airport and caught an Eastern Airlines flight to San Juan.

When they got to San Juan, they took a cab and went straight to the Borinquen Hotel. They all registered for and stayed in one room. It was then that Vasler told the other two of the final plans for transporting the cocaine back to Minneapolis after they took delivery of the goods.

"First," Vasler said, "I don't know exactly when the shipment is going to reach here, it will be in the next day of two. In the meantime, we need to get to the airport and see how baggage is checked in, and what kind they have a tendency to inspect. I'm told that they examine all pieces for agriculture products. We'll see."

"What's our cut going to be?" asked Douglas.

"Now that we've got this far," answered Vasler, "I can tell you that your share will be $15,000 each. I think that is fair enough, in as much as I've been paying all your expenses.

You've been living it up pretty good!"

Both Thomas and Douglas thought their share could be a bit more but didn't want to argue and possibly be cut out with nothing, perhaps even left stranded in Puerto Rico. They knew the temper of Vasler.

"You guys are going to check out of this hotel tomorrow morning. I've got a room reserved for you at the Buena Vista Guest House. You will stay there until I call you and let you know what the next step will be."

"Why's that?" asked Thomas.

Irritated, Vasler said, "Because I said so, that's why. And besides, like I said before, the people I'm working with on the other end want to limit the number of people who see them and who could identify them at a later time. It's a lot safer for you, too. These people can be very rough, dangerous, if the need arises!"

That afternoon the three went to the airport and watched as baggage was carried though the entry gates and checked in.

It was true, all baggage was examined for agriculture products. After a piece was examined, a strip of tape was placed over the opening of that bag, showing that, the bag, had been checked. Once the bag had been examined, it was given back to the traveler who was then free to carry the baggage throughout the airport prior to checking in for their particular flight.

Back at the Buena Vista Guest House, they decided that the simplest way to go was to carry four suitcases. Two would have the cocaine and two would have clothing and miscellaneous items. The two with clothes would be passed through the agriculture inspection and the tape, of course, applied by the inspectors. That tape would then be carefully removed and placed on the two containing the cocaine.

They were buoyed by the thought of how easy this would work out. They even found a nearby men's room where the transfer of the tape could be performed, with the first two pieces of baggage going through for another agriculture examination.

They felt so good about their pending act of deception that they decided to celebrate, although Vasler made sure that they didn't drink too much, because, "I want us to all have our wits about us when we make this move."

Vasler then went back to the Borinquen Hotel to wait, instructing the other two not to leave their room, not even to eat, because when he called, they will have to move fast. "You can have room service, I will pay."

After three days, on the evening of February 9th, Vasler called his buddies to advise them that "The bubble gum has started to show up. Do you guys want to come to my place? I think there may be a collectors card or two with the delivery."

Douglas and Thomas took a cab, and when they got to Vasler's room, he said that he already had taken delivery of six kilo's and that more was coming. They looked to where he was pointing, under the bed, and saw the packages.

"A girl named Debbie brought this," said Vasler, "She's able to carry a couple pounds at a time in her purse, so it's not going to take too long. when she comes back, you guys are going to have to go into the john. She doesn't want anyone to see Her."

A short time later, after a knock on the door, Douglas and Thomas doing as they had been told,still could hear through the closed door Vasler's conversation with a female with a heavy New York City accent. She left in about five minutes.

371

When they reentered the room they saw six more bags of cocaine on the desk. Vasler told them that delivery was made by Debbie, the fat girl from New York that they had met when partying in Cartagena. Their memory of this was obscured by the coke and drinking they had gone through that day.

Vasler explained, "Seems that she's in love with one of the Colombian's and will do anything for him. He's using her to run errands like this. The stuff is coming into Puerto Rico on a pleasure boat.

A steward from the cruise ship is the one smuggling the coke into San Juan. They don't check the ships crew too carefully, particularly the ones who make this port of call on a regular basis."

Thomas suddenly got jittery, thinking of many complications this venture might lead to and asked to be excused. He actually felt sick to his stomach.

Vasler said, "That's okay, you can go back to the Buena Vista and wait, we'll go get something to eat later, it will settle your stomach."

Douglas and Vasler set up a portable testing kit which Vasler had purchased in a head shop down the street from the Hotel and proceeded to test the coke which had been delivered thus far. The samples tested positive.

About an hour later a knock on the door caused Douglas to return to the bathroom, whereupon another delivery was made. The same female voice was heard.

Subsequently, two more deliveries were made, for a total of five. In all, approximately fifteen kilos were accepted by Vasler.

When they had completed testing the other packages, Vasler put the coke in a laundry bag and placed it in the room's kitchenette. They then went to the hotel bar, on the top floor, to discuss strategy. They drank until the bar closed, forgetting Vasler's own dictum that they must have a clear head. Douglas caught a cab back to the Buena Vista.

In the morning Vasler packed the cocaine in two of the suitcases they had bought the day before. In order to keep them out of sight, he loosened the ceiling air vent cover just inside the entry door to his room, got up on a chair, and hoisted the suitcases up and into the opening.

*Eli J. Miletich*

After replacing the ceiling vent cover, Vasler went down to the hotel restaurant for some breakfast.

When he returned to his room, he unlocked the door and was immediately grabbed and pulled in by plainclothes officers who identified themselves as San Juan police.

The ceiling air vent was missing and he saw that his two suitcases were on the bed in an open position.

"Where's your search warrant?" demanded Vasler.

"Look smart ass," one of the officers said, "In circumstances like this, we don't need a search warrant. A maid comes in the room to clean up and make the bed. She noticed the air vent ajar, got a chair, looked up in there and found the suitcases. She called us. We opened the suitcases and found the cocaine. You are under arrest for Possession of Cocaine with Intent to Sell."

Strange, thought Vasler, this guy doesn't even look like a Latino, and he sure doesn't have a Puerto Rican accent.

Douglas and Thomas had checked out of the Buena Vista and were in the Borinquen lobby, about to go to Vaslers room, when they saw him being escorted, in handcuffs, by police, out of the hotel and into a waiting police car.

"Let's get the hell our of here, quick," said Douglas.

They immediately went to the airport, made reservations for the very next flight to Miami and were waiting at the gate when a small squad of police approached and placed them under arrest.

They were questioned for over four hours, not volunteering any information or knowledge of what Vasler was involved in. They maintained that they were on an antique hunting trip which they combined with a vacation. It, the story, was something they had talked about when they were alone and not with Vasler.

Lacking probable cause, the hotel room was in Vaslers name, the police had to release them. They quickly caught the first cab they saw, returned to the airport and booked seats for passage to Duluth, via Miami and Minneapolis, sweating all the way.

Vasler, after several days of interrogation by the Puerto Rican police, now joined by DEA agents, was fully cognizant of the solid case against him. He was informed that the DEA was going to waive any jurisdictional rights to him. That he would be tried in a Puerto Rico court, and when convicted, he would serve out his entire term in a dingy, rat infested, homosexual inhabited, Puerto Rican prison.

Vasler gave a verbal statement that named important people, professional people, back in Minneapolis, to whom he had intended to bring the cocaine. He was only to receive a commission and a small amount of the cocaine.

He described a network of runners and mules who were used to transport quantities ranging from one pound to forty and fifty pounds.

He told of how young females were approached in bars and other hangouts, dated, encouraged to try coke and even heroin. When they were part of the 'in' crowd, the women were then convinced that they could have a steady supply of drugs and in fact, get rich, by becoming mules, i.e., couriers.

Several women from Duluth, including an educator, and a Tribune employee, were involved, with the most common mode of transportation being vaginal concealment. Names were flowing from this scared subject and he told agents that he would reduce his statement to writing and sign it, if they would assure him a federal trial so that he could serve time on the mainland in a federal prison. With the blessing of a U.S. Attorney, such assurances were given.

Vasler wanted to rest for a bit before starting again, so they all took a break.

How do you know when an attorney is lying? Here we go again.

Late that same afternoon, and before the agents could get back to Vasler, an attorney arrived from Minneapolis and insisted on seeing Vasler. His name was Ide Pizdu.

During the earlier interrogation, Vasler had given his attorneys name, but this guy wasn't the one. Rather, he was one of the important people, one of the professional people Vasler had named as being involved.

"I am filling in for Marc Vaslers attorney and if you deny me, you would be denying my client his right to counsel." he hissed.

The DEA agents decided to take a chance rather than get into a constitutional challenge later and allowed this attorney, Pizdu, to see Vasler.

When that attorney departed, heading back to Minneapolis, Vasler was approached by the DEA agents for the written statement.

Visibly shaken and ashen gray, Vasler refused to talk, much less write anything. When asked what the attorney had talked to him about, Vasler would only say, "Nothing, I just want to do my time. I don't want to die young."

Having pity for this man, the U.S. Attorney, as recommended by the DEA, decided to try him in federal court after all. He pled guilty and was sentenced to the maximum time in a federal prison in Illinois. By the way, he was not represented in court by the attorney, Pizdu.

Pizdu, a sometimes target of local, state and federal law enforcement in the Twin Cities area, continues to practice law unscathed, apparently because of his strong connections and the fear that he can place in the heart of anyone who might be tempted to implicate him.

Another case, similar to Marc Vasler, involved a conversation overheard by an informant, #68, and to which the informant joined in without an invitation.

I got a call from #68 one spring afternoon and he asked if we would be interested in buying some cocaine which was almost one hundred percent pure. "This stuff hasn't been stepped on a bit. You know what that means don't you?" he asked.

"Yeah, I do, where did you come across that kind of stuff?" I asked.

We were aware that cocaine with that purity was a rarity this far into the country. Usually, when 'coke' is smuggled, the first hands that touch it dilute it, which the dopers refer to by various names, including cutting or, stepping on it. An innocuous white powder of the same density as cocaine was usually used. The more times the cocaine was stepped on the greater the profit margin for the handlers.

#68 briefed me on what he believed to be a sure thing. "I was in the Downtown Post Office yesterday, sending my mother a Mother's Day card and, when I was doing the address, I heard two guys standing at the table talking about a big score one of them had made. I looked up and knew the one doing all the talking, a guy from Minneapolis who comes to town a lot. The other guy was a scuzzball from Duluth who I've seen around, but not a particular friend of mine.

The guy from Duluth wasn't interested, so I jumped into the conversation. We were the only people standing at the table in the middle of the Post Office lobby. Anyway, the guy from Minneapolis recognized me and said, 'cool, do you want to buy some?' Of course, I told him yes, but that I didn't want to try any stuff that wasn't stepped on. A guy could get awful sick or even die if it wasn't diluted and he wasn't used to stuff that strong, even in a small amount.

He agreed and I bought a quarter gram of which I told him I was going to cut myself before using any. I've got it now if you want to test it, but I need to be refunded for my expenses."

I said, "Tell you what, I'll send Denny Lepak and Mike Anderson to meet you and get the coke. They will refund you. If the stuff turns out to be what your Minneapolis friend says it is,

I'm sure we'll want to look into this further. Do you know where to get in touch with this guy?"

"Sure, I've got his number in the Cities and the number of the woman he comes here to see about once a week. He said to try him at his Twin Cities apartment first."

When Lepak and Anderson returned to the office, we quick tested a minute portion of the white powder on our Valtox Field Testing Kit and got the fastest chemical reaction we had ever seen. The only problem with a Valtox test is that it is only for preliminary tests in the field. It is semi reliable, and doesn't test for the degree of purity.

Ron Swanson, resident Drug Enforcement Agency Agent, was called and came over from his office in the Federal Building.

Swanson, a native of Minneapolis, had been with the DEA for about twelve years when he was transferred from his most recent assignment in Toronto. A very street wise agent who thought like a cop, and because of that trait he was able to relate to cops in every jurisdiction to which he was assigned, or had occasion to work with.

He made a study of each subject and informant he was ever involved with and, as a result, turned in some of the best cases the DEA had come up with for years.

The flaming red hair of his youth was already showing visible streaks of gray but, as a former athlete, at five feet ten inches, one hundred seventy pounds, he kept himself in the shape of a nineteen year old.

"Look guys," he said, "We need to send this to a lab where they can confirm if our suspicions are on track. Let me sign the Property Transfer Sheet and I'll send this to our Chicago lab right away."

Two days later Swanson came into our office beaming.

"Guess what, guys?" He had a look on his face like the proverbial cat that had just swallowed the canary.

"Don't tell us," I said, "the stuff was one hundred percent corn starch."

"What in hell was it?" said Lepak, "Don't keep us guessing.

"Ninety six percent pure cocaine. I've already talked to my boss, the regional director in Chicago, and they want us to follow this up. They feel that this has to involve some heavy people. When can I talk to the informant?"

"Screw you federal agent Swanson, we're not going to turn any snitch over to you so that you can steal him from us," I kidded him, "We know how guys like you and John Magarac run off with informants when we introduce them to you." He was familiar with the incident involving ATF Agent Magarac.

He came back quickly. "Okay, then it will be a cold day in hell when I arrange for informant 'buy money' from my bosses for your operation here. Besides, where do you get off lumping me in the same bag with that donkey, Magarac?"

We all laughed and got down to serious business.

Ron was to be introduced by #68 to the guy from Minneapolis as a Canadian. It always seemed to be a good cover for someone about to embark on an undercover effort to be labeled as from Canada, what with our close proximity to the border.

As a legitimate businessman from Thunder Bay, Ron was going to lay down a story that he had other professional and business associates in his city who had need for the product on a recreational basis.

The first part of this operation went off like it was scripted. Ron Bought a quarter ounce from the dealer from Minneapolis. He laid down the story that if his customers were satisfied after he had cut it once, perhaps twice, then he would maybe want to buy more.

The next few buys were for a half ounce at a time. Each buy was quickly sent to Chicago for testing. The lab results were astounding. Ninety five percent pure one time, ninety four percent the next.

Naturally, Ron Swanson's superiors at the regional level in Chicago were very interested in moving on to the next level. Approval was granted for an even larger buy.

#68 was no longer needed as a middle man, in that Ron had gained the confidence of the Minneapolis dealer, a guy who had been using the fictitious name of Eddie Felsen but, it was learned through surveillance and other means, was a fired junior high school teacher named Jerry Pryor.

At his next meeting with Pryor, Ron had the necessary 'flash' money to prove his capability to produce the required cash.

We also were concerned with the possibility of a rip off, in other words a reverse sting, so our surveillance of the meeting was more than doubled. Ron did not want to wear a wire, in case he was patted down.

That buy also went off smooth.

We were resigned to be patient, recognizing that it would take some time, at least three to four weeks, for the 'Canadian' to sell his inventory and then call for more.

After a month had lapsed, Swanson got in touch with Pryor and made arrangements for a buy of one pound of cocaine. He laid down a story that his market was expanding in Canada and that he may be in for larger quantities in the very near future.

Pryor was eager to accommodate him and assured Ron that his contact in New Orleans concurred. This was the first time that the next level had been mentioned.

That meeting and buy also went smooth and, while they were downing a beer after their business had been concluded,

Swanson casually said, "What do I have to do if the demand gets so strong that I need to buy some kilos, can I get it through you?"

"No way," answered Pryor, "My man in New Orleans would have to do that. He's closest to the Colombians. But, they will want to be sure that you have the cash."

Swanson thought for a minute and said, "No problem, but I'm not going to carry around that kind of money in public, too ripe for a rip off. Tell you what, if it turns out that I need to expand I'll let you know, but first I will put the money in a safety deposit box in one of the banks in this area. I can show it to you here, and then I'll know that there will be no hanky panky. Fair enough?"

"Sounds like good thinking to me," answered Pryor.

In another six weeks, Ron called Pryor in Minneapolis and asked what it would take to buy twenty four kilos.Ron gave him a number to a 'cool' phone in his office, a phone just answered with a 'yeah' or 'what's up?'

Three and one half hours later Pryor called. "Ninety five thousand for twenty four kilos."

Swanson whistled, "Whew, pretty steep."

"Look, they know that you are stepping on it at least three times, maybe four, so they say that you can triple or quadruple your investment. They say that's their bottom line for uncut stuff. Take it or leave it! I'm just the messenger, although I'll get a small commission if the deal comes off."

Arrangements were made for Pryor to come to Duluth, meet with Swanson the first night in town, then the next morning, at eleven, meet again at the Superior National Bank in Superior, Wisconsin, across the bay, where Ron would show him the money.

The next morning, after checking the area for any allies of Pryor, Gene Sisto and I set up shop in an old beat up VW van, parked in a super market parking lot across the intersection, diagonally, from the bank.

Beautiful. The sun was shining bright, lighting up the front of the bank and the setting even included a large clock over the entrance, displaying the time, and above that, the name of the bank.

*Eli J. Miletich*

At precisely eleven A.M ., Pryor arrived. They shook hands and stood in front of a bank chatting.

We were snapping photos with a telephoto camera.

When they emerged from the bank, Pryor said, "I'll let them know that you're good for the cash, but the guy in New Orleans will probably want to meet you. Can you fly down there if he asks?"

"For this kind of deal, naturally!"

Pryor drove back to Duluth across the Richard Bong High Bridge spanning the inner bay of the Duluth-Superior harbor, and from there back south to Minneapolis, unaware that he had company on Interstate 35 all the way to his apartment. We had to be sure that he did not have any of his friends on counter surveillance.

Three days later Pryor called Swanson and arrangements were made for Ron to fly to New Orleans with Pryor.

Swanson had to get approval for the trip from his superiors. Normally, an introduction would have occurred to another agent from Louisiana as a partner of Ron's, who would then follow through on the case, however since we all believed that

388

continuity was important so that the whole thing wouldn't be blown, we did impress that on the Chicago folks, and they agreed.

In New Orleans, Ron was introduced to the source, actually a husband and wife team, and after about a three hour interview they told him that he would have to go to Bogota to receive the cocaine, because he was getting such a good deal, further, he would have to make arrangements for transporting it back to the States. They would instruct him on how this could be done with ease, though.

This far into it, Swanson presumed that his bosses would want him to follow it to a conclusion, so he agreed that he would go, but with a defensive posture, he assured them that he would leave for Bogota at an undisclosed time.

"Please understand that I don't want to be traveling with such a large sum of cash, with you or anyone else knowing of the time of my leaving or from where." Being in the business, they said they understood.

"Give me a number to call when I get to Bogota and I'll make arrangements when I get there."

389

*Eli J. Miletich*

Swanson waited until he returned to Duluth before he called Chicago, in the event he was tailed. His bosses had reservations but they approved, indicating that they would arrange for DEA agents in Bogota to put him under surveillance for his security as soon as he deplaned there.

Three days later, Ron went to Miami, from there to Bogota. He called the number he was given and a time was set for delivery that night. They would call him back at his hotel room to give him the place.

He went into the men's room at the airport as had been previously worked out, met with a DEA agent who passed him a very microscopic bug and gave him a verbal signal to utter when and if the cocaine was in fact delivered. That meeting lasted less than twenty seconds.

Swanson checked into his previously reserved hotel and waited for the call. It came at 7:15 P.M. and he was given directions to the place for the meeting. It was only about a half mile from his hotel. He was to be there at 8:30 P.M. sharp.

At the appointed time, Swanson arrived in a rental car in a rundown center city of Bogota. He later described all of Bogota as rundown.

He knew that DEA people were somewhere out there on surveillance and, according to the brief conversation he had previously with the agent at the airport, several Bogota city cops as well as Colombian national police. He just hoped that his peers had given the locals a thorough description of him, in case anything went wrong.

He didn't have to wait long. In less than two minutes, a shiny black Mercedes pulled up behind Swansons rental car. Two well dressed guys, looked to be in their early thirties, got out of the back seat and walked up to Ron's vehicle.

Their English was passable. "Are you waiting for some packages senor?"

"Yes."

"Follow me," The one who seemed to be in charge said as he turned and walked back to the rear of the Mercedes.

Swanson glanced into the front seat of the Mercedes as he passed, and noticed that the driver was holding an eight by eleven black and white glossy photo of him, not attempting to conceal it from view. "The son of bitches," he thought, "They had someone taking photos when the meeting took place in New Orleans."

There were no introductions.

When he and the two Colombians were standing at the rear of the car, one of them rapped on the trunk lid and the guy behind the wheel leaned forward, pushed a button on the dash, and the trunk lid slowly opened.

There on the floor of the trunk were a number, he assumed twenty four tightly wrapped, plastic, packages.

The signal: "Wow, will you look at all them green apples!"

At that, all agents were supposed to rush out of their hiding places and put the suspects under arrest.

It didn't work out that way, however. A couple of the Bogota police immediately commenced firing their weapons, apparently to signal the cocaine traffickers. Fortunately, the DEA agents and their Colombian counterparts quickly disarmed the locals, got off a few rounds of their own into the air as they rushed the car, and the arrest of the three suspects from the Mercedes was accomplished.

Swanson, unarmed when the shooting started, described the next thirty seconds as sheer pandemonium and fright. Until his peers had things under control, he said, "You never saw a guy fall to the pavement so fast and blend with the curb as I did in that instant with the bullets flying overhead." Small wonder.

It turned out that the two Bogota cops had been suspected of collaborating with cocaine dealers for some time and a decision had been made, without Swanson knowing it, that this would be the time to check them out. They failed the test and were charged under Colombian law, convicted and sentenced to stiff prison terms.

The guys from the Mercedes were also convicted, served less than six months in a resort like compound. Important positions in one of the cartels, it seems.

Back in the States a federal grand jury indicted the New Orleans husband and wife team along with Pryor. The New Orleans couple were convicted.

*Eli J. Miletich*

At his arraignment Pryor denied any involvement, insisting that he had never been to Superior, Wisconsin in his life, and only rarely to Duluth. Naturally, Swanson's testimony, supported by excellent photos of the meeting in front of the Superior National Bank, secured his conviction.

The Drug Enforcement Agency headquarters sent letters of commendation to our department with the usual citations included, but the fact is that except for our initial contact with the informant, it was DEA Agent Ron Swanson who carried the case from start to finish at great risk to his own safety. A real hero in the war on drugs, a war that no one is sure we are winning.

Chapter Twenty Five

It isn't only ordinary citizens who can succumb to the temptations that surround us in our everyday lives. Cops are among the most vulnerable.

I had just shut my office door, telling secretary Dolores Pohjola to take messages on all calls. The day had been a busy one and I wanted a chance to put my feet up on the desk and review notes I had taken during a budget strategy session in the Mayor's Conference Room with the other eight City Department Directors.

I had successfully argued, even though the crime rate had gone down for the fifth straight year, that we could only maintain the high level of safety and security for our citizens if we were allowed to strengthen our staff by the addition of more officers on patrol. I knew that was not entirely true, because, as the saying goes, "even with a cop on every corner, there will still be crime."

The directors of the Library, Public works and Planning Department's had to put their plans for expansion on hold for a

Eli J. Miletich

year, but the efficiencies and consolidations of positions on our department, in recent years, was finally being recognized and paying off.

A knock at the door and the entry of Deputy Chief Gene Sisto and Detective Bureau Inspector Fred Sowl with solemn looks on their faces told me that something serious was up.

"Got a couple minutes, Eli?" Asked Gene.

"Yeah, what's happening?"

"Fred just briefed me on a problem that's come up in Narco-Vice. There's a large amount of money missing from the Narco Buy Fund." Said Gene.

"How in hell can that be, do you mean that there are no receipts for undercover or informant drug purchases?"

"It's not that" said Sowl, "There's about fourteen hundred dollars missing from the locked file drawer where the money is kept and the last guy who was known to have signed out for any money for an informant was Rod."

"Has anyone talked with him about it?" I asked

"Yes, but he denies knowing what happened to the money. He did sign out for about fifty dollars to refund a snitch for a buy

396

of a small amount of marijuana. Looks like another buy by the informant will establish him solid so that he, the snitch, will be able to bring along an undercover agent the next time around. But Rod maintains that when he took out the $50 two nights ago, the $1,400 was in the locked file." Explained Fred.

"How about the worksheets of the other guys working in Narco-Vice? Is there any indication that any of them had reason to go into the Buy Fund file?" I asked.

"No," replied Fred, "We've checked that out and every guy has been busy on other cases and would have had no reason to go into the fund."

"Who's talked to Rod? And what does his sergeant say about it?"

"I have and one of the lieutenants, but he insists that he doesn't know what happened to the money. His sergeant has been off sick for over two weeks.We've even taken out all the drawers and looked the whole cabinet over."

"Where is Rod now?"

"He will be coming in shortly for the afternoon shift." Said Sisto.

"Gene, have a talk with him and see what you can find out. We're going to have to put every guy in Narco-Vice on the lie box to get to the bottom of this. And, tear up the carpeting in that office if necessary. The damn money didn't just fly away!" I insisted.

The money in the Buy Fund came from two sources; a certain amount budgeted by the City, and monies allocated to the state and cities from the federal criminal justice system in its' so called war on drugs. It is used in order to establish that suspects are indeed involved in the sales of controlled substances, i.e., illegal drugs.

There was and is a carefully designed process whereby any money spent is signed for by either the undercover agent making the buy or with a simple number by the informant. Each informant has a number in the Narco-Vice confidential files. All such buys are logged on daily worksheets and require a report on the particular suspect detailing the transaction. The drugs are also inventoried with a property report left documenting same.

About thirty minutes later, Gene Sisto came into my office and said, "You know what, after Rod reported in for work, I went to the Narco-Vice office and told him I wanted to talk with him but we first looked in the file cabinet, even behind the drawer, and of all things, there were a bunch of bills, fourteen hundred dollars worth, stuck there. Only thing, they were all crisp new bills. Something is weird, but he says he doesn't know anything about it.

The money wasn't in the locked metal box where it should have been and usually is."

"How about if you bring him up here and we both can talk with him. Right now, with this money turning up just after he comes in to work, I can't believe that it was overlooked before, and you say it's crisp and new looking. Sounds not too good. We need to talk with him."

"O.K.," Said Gene, "I'll go down to Narco-vice and bring him right up."

In about five minutes they came in, Rod having a very hang dog look about him.

*Eli J. Miletich*

Here was a six foot, three inch Viet Nam War hero, wounded twice as a Navy combat medic serving with the Marines, nervous as hell and here I was, about to question the guy who had once saved me from getting shot in the back while going after a prison escapee.

"How's it going, Rod. I don't see you much in the years since I left Narco?" I said, in an effort at small talk.

"Not so good, if you want to know the truth."

"The truth is what I asked to talk with you about, Rod. I want to tell you up front that I believe that you know more about this missing money than you have been telling the guys. Under the Union Agreement with the City, you have a right to have a union observer with you at this time."

He shocked us. "I don't need anyone from the union, I took it."

"What? I said.

"I said, I took it because I've been into heavy gambling with pull tabs and lost more than I earn. I went to a bank and took out a loan to replace the cash I took."

213

I was flabbergasted, Gene was flabbergasted, and since we were not investigators anymore, I quickly said "Rod, will you take a seat in the secretary's office, the Assistant Chief and I need to talk."

Rod did as asked and when the door was closed, I said to Gene, "Well, you know, we need to contact the County Attorney about criminal prosecution and the City Attorney about termination action under Civil Service Rules. We'd better get Fred back up here so we can tell him about Rod's comments then he can assign someone from the Detective Bureau to follow through on this.

Gene called Fred back up to my office and after he heard about Rod's admission, we called him back in and he sat in a chair opposite my desk.

"Rod," I matter of factly told him. "We're not going to talk further about this matter other than this: The Inspector is going to assign some people to take your statement and we want you to be 100 per cent truthful. Also, the Deputy Chief is going to contact the County Attorney's office about initiating criminal charges because, as you know, this constitutes a felony. We are also going to notify the City Attorney's office so they can prepare the necessary papers for termination from employment. As a union representative, I'm sure you're aware that according to the rules, you will be placed on leave of absence with pay until the whole matter has been adjudicated."

"I'm aware of that."

"Okay, as of now you are suspended pending further action by the City Attorney and the Civil Service Board. But, I want you to go down to the Detective Bureau with Inspector Sowl and he will have someone there talk with you and get your statement.

The County Attorney will decide later whether there needs to be incarceration at this point until you appear in court, but I doubt it, in as much as you have your roots in this city, have a family here and have freely made an admission. You can go with the the Inspector now."

After Rod had left, I turned to Deputy Chief Sisto and said, " Remember when I testified before the legislative committee which was studying the legalization of pull tab gambling for so-called charitable organizations. I was one of the very few people in law enforcement who was against it. My testimony was that it would lead to bankruptcy and crime by people who lose their paychecks. Well, a couple of our attorney friends have told me of the upsurge in bankruptcies because of pull tab gambling, but little did I ever dream that one of the first people to go down the tubes because of it would be a cop, especially a friend and one we've worked with closely."

I think we both felt like crying. This was a man who had saved my life!

The interview by detectives with Rod brought to light another series of thefts by him. As Secretary-Treasurer of the Police Welfare Association and the Union, he had been making out checks to himself for no valid or authorized reason, and was subsequently charged with an additional felony count.

At his trial the judge, apparently taking into consideration Rod's military record and, up to the present his excellent police service, sentenced him to ten years probation and ordered to pay back the police department and the two associations. The Civil Service Board followed up on my petition that his employment be terminated.

Rod voluntarily entered a compulsive gambling treatment program in Maryland for six weeks, a program modeled after that of a similar one for treatment of alcoholics.

Rod, one of those unfortunates who learned the hard way that gambling can be addictive, got his life back in order, worked for several years in the community as a counselor for people who suffer from the same addiction.

When you accept a position in law enforcement you must assume a persona not too much unlike that of a member of the clergy. You must be clean as a hounds tooth. People look at you in a different light and think that you should make no mistakes or suffer from poor judgment. They're wrong, we are only human, but the test is to resist temptation.

One of the saddest of all my law enforcement experiences.

Chapter Twenty Six

## October 13

Bob Harvey called Pat Alexander and said, "More Good news. My buddies in San Diego have been diligently monitoring a tracer on the Smith family phone for three days and as a result of their saddened, but voluntary, cooperation, they learned that Smith was staying at a motel in Hartford, Connecticut. He's been there since October 11th. They have already passed this on to our Hartford FBI office and the Hartford PD.

My San Diego guys also learned, from the family, that Michael Smith had disappeared, then shipped out on an ocean freighter over a year ago when a man he knew was gunned down and then stabbed to death.

Smith left California on September 20th, apparently skipping out on a sentencing for a burglary conviction. His parents had also tossed him out of their home.

Smith was in the upper echelon of a San Diego drug ring that ran an illegal methamphetamine, speed, lab, as well as cocaine trafficking. It seems that he was implicated in a drug related double homicide, he being the shooter. They've learned that a second suspect in the killings was now out to kill him."

"Whew", said Alexander. "I'll bring my bosses up to date, great work, Bob"

"No, great work, Pat and all the guys on the Duluth PD. The guy should be in custody within the hour, and, I'll call you as soon as I get the word."

Fifty minutes later, Bob Harvey called and said, "Got 'em, no resistance either. It worked out great, they put together an arrest task force with the Hartford PD and took him without an incident. I suppose you guys will want to extradite?"

"No doubt, but we'll have to check with the bosses here and the County Attorneys office. Thanks again, Bob. Great team work!"

Detective Bureau Inspector Fred Sowl and Sergeant Pat Alexander came to my office to brief me.

"I suppose you'll want to get a junket out of this by going to Hartford to pick him up if he's extradited." I said to Pat. We all roared.

"Well, I hadn't really thought of it, but it's a good idea, and I've already talked with John DeSanto over at the County Attorneys office and he is preparing extradition papers. Maybe the guy will waive extradition and speed it up."

"Give a call to the Hartford cops right now and see when you can go out there." I said.

A quick call and Pat learned that Michael Smith had already stated that he would waive extradition, so Alexander made reservations for an early morning flight the next day for himself and another detective.

In Hartford, when the vehicle had been processed by technicians, they confirmed that Roxanna's body had been carried in the rear of the Toyota. Her blood was found on the carpet floor, and the side panels. A decorative bead from the sweater she was wearing when her body was found in Duluth was on the back seat floor.

Flying to Hartford the next morning, with a connecting flight in Chicago, Alexander learned that Smith was found with Roxanna's car, her credit cards and check book in his possession.

He was told that Smith also had the credit cards stolen from the woman in Indianapolis as well as Suhada Rossi's cards from Minnisuing in Wisconsin and a Boulder motel room key.

Alexander met Michael Smith in the Hartford jail and asked him if he would submit to an interview. "Yeah," He replied, and since he was in custody, before proceeding with the interview, Pat read him his rights as per the Supreme Court Miranda ruling.

"Why don't you tell me about that young woman that you came across in Boulder, Colorado a couple weeks ago?" Asked Pat.

"It was this way. I was on the run from San Diego and when passing through Boulder, I used up most of what little cash I started out with in renting a motel for one night. After I checked out in the afternoon, I had supper at a small, cheap, restaurant and then stopped at this noisy bar for a few drinks. Just when I was leaving around ten thirty or eleven, I noticed this short, cute, black haired gal leaving after buying a pack of cigarettes. As she was getting into her vehicle, a Toyota station wagon, in the parking lot, I approached her and asked for directions to the highway. When she turned to point , I grabbed her by the mouth and pushed her into her vehicle. She tried to struggle, so I punched her and knocked her out. I slid behind the wheel and drove to a side road, parked and dragged her out of the vehicle and let her fall on the ground. I looked around and found a broken tree branch and picked it up and hit her in the head five or six times. She died right there.

I was broke and the station wagon was an easy way to gain transportation, so I placed her in the back of the wagon, wrapped her in blankets and some laundry she had piled up back there. I drove east from there toward Fort Morgan.

In Fort Morgan, at a gas station, I came across a guy who was heading to a lake in northern Wisconsin and he asked me if I was in no hurry did I want to make a few bucks and help him close up a cabin for the winter. Some doctor in Southern California owned it and the guy, a contractor friend of his was doing him a favor. One night, while at the cabin, I decided to take a ride, went to Duluth and dropped the body in some high grass along a stretch of road up on the other side of the city's hills."

Later, back in Duluth, Pat described Smith as conversing in a calm, dispassionate manner, as though he was never involved in anything and was removed from the incident completely, as if describing a movie or play he had seen. The following day, after waiving extradition, Smith was returned to Duluth by Alexander and the other officer.

The Roxanna Livingston-Voorsanger murder case set a legal precedent in Minnesota. The State Supreme Court ruled that when a slaying occurs in another state and the body is brought to Minnesota, the suspect can't be tried in Minnesota. And, since the Deputy Medical Examiner had determined that she had been dead for two days before her body was found, Colorado had jurisdiction.

On his court appearance in St. Louis County Court in Duluth, Smith waived extradition and was returned to the County Jail to await a of couple sheriff's deputies from Colorado who then took him back there for trial.

The San Diego Police Department renewed a stalled murder investigation in their city which resulted in double homicide charges being placed against Smith there. It is alleged that he and a partner killed two men, execution style, believing them to be informants. They are believed to have slit their throats, then shot them.

Michael Edward Smith chose not to be extradited to California, preferring Colorado, a non capital punishment state, whereas California has the death penalty.

Smith was convicted in Colorado for the murder of Roxanna Livingston-Voorsanger and sentenced to 20 years in prison.

The State of California has a detainer on him, which means that they want him for trial when he gets out in Colorado. Let's hope California remembers.

The Roxanna Livingston-Voorsanger homicide investigation, coordinated by Sergeant Pat Alexander, started with only that match book as evidence and involved superior cooperation by eighteen law enforcement agencies in ten states.

It, the investigation, was officially recognized, after the conviction of Michael Edward Smith, with a Departmental Commendation Award for Alexander and the officers assisting him which said, in part:

*Eli J. Miletich*

*"The Police Department Citation Board, in it's review of recommendations for the Commendation Award, has adjudged that the award be granted to the following officers of the Investigative Division, particularly Sergeant Patrick Alexander, along with Lieutenants Beverly Ecklund, John Hall, Donneta Wickstrom, and Sergeants, John Kalenowski. Chris Kucera, Mike Anderson, retired Sergeant Harold Abrams, and officer Barry Brooks.*

*In addition to the officers of our department being commended, three other individuals should be mentioned as performing an outstanding job toward the solution of this case. They include FBI Special Agent in Charge Robert Harvey, Dawn Kast of the City Graphics Department and Secretarial Specialist Ann Brooks.*

*On Wednesday, April 12, 1989, Michael Edward Smith of San Diego, was convicted and sentenced at Fort Morgan, Colorado to twenty rears in prison for the killing of Roxanna Livingston-Voorsanger. She was believed to have been killed in Colorado and her body dumped in a ditch on Arrowhead Road where she was found, on October 1, 1987. There were no*

412

*witnesses and no identification was found, just a matchbook on*

*her person. Through a concerted, timely, persistent, thorough*

*and far reaching investigation, coordinated and directed by*

*Sergeant Alexander, involving many agencies, the case was*

*brought to a successful conclusion.*

*This ending to the investigation brings credit to the entire*

*law enforcement community, but especially to the Duluth Police*

*Department. It is with pride that this Commendation is*

*awarded."*

———————————————————

Oh, by the way, in case you didn't already know it, the
answer to the question about attorneys in Chapters 17 and 24,
is—— *"When his lips are moving"*

Printed in the United States
1462000001B/250-267